Synopsis

will give an insight to life in Scotland during the late 17th
centuries. Various books have been written on specific
ork has brought everything together. There are
ooks on the subject of Bonnie Prince Charlie and the
. This is understandable due to the charismatic figures
d it is only right that they have demanded attention from
In making that statement it has to be emphasized that
just clearly romantic fiction based on some facts.
ard during the 17th and 18th centuries as there was no
for the poor yet the Highlands had a social structure that
heir own. Social assimilation was ascetically deficient
ghland line and people in the Lowlands had little
g of how these people lived. The position of a clan chief's
ansmen will be explained as it was then and now.
e Highlands will also be explored covering what folk ate,
music and general way of life. Political aspects such as the
me and the Treaty of Union brought chaos into Scotland.
he implications of these and what did the Scot's do? This
lighted in chapter IV.
ans did not exist until the early 1800s, this book with detail
the dress and weaponry of a Highlander and why they
and garb till the proscription in 1747 after the battle of
Ruffians, rogues and rascals have always been present in
ty. What was crime during this period in Scotland? Some
nishments will also be brought to the reader's attention. The
n 1689-1719 will be outlined for the reader.

Scottish Cul...

During the late 17th and early 18th centuries

By Norman C Milne

With an appendix on Tartan by Gordon Nicolson

Front cover from left to right back row Norman C Milne, David
Cunningham, Peter Chambers, Ian Logan, Alistair MacNeill, Colin
Innes, Paul Power and Colin Rutherford.
Front row, Stuart Morris, Raymond Morris The Laird of Balgonie
Castle, Matthew Donnachie, Michael Corby and Robert Jensen.
The front cover picture was taken within the grounds of Balgonie
Castle.

To Hilary
Hope you enjoy
All the best.
Norman.

Published by Norman Milne

Publishing partner: Paragon Publishing, Rothersthorpe

First published 2010

ISBN 978-1-899820-79-5

Book design, layout and production management by Into Print
www.intoprint.net

Printed and bound in UK and USA by Lightning Source

Fo

The Highlands of Scotland and i͏͏
authors, not simply from Scotlan͏
The Highlands have been the sub͏
also popular writers over the cent͏
about the Scottish Highlands. One͏
thought that nothing more could b͏
history. Norman Milne's book now͏
for the fortunate reader. Whether h͏
highland dress or customs, it is clea͏
the subject on which he writes. No͏
Highlands and its history for his enti͏
subject exudes from every page of S͏
which should be read by everyone w͏
Highlands but also Scotland as a nati͏
straight-forward style. It should find͏
can be thoroughly recommended. I ho͏
gets as much pleasure as I did. I wish͏
deserves.

Professor Francis McManus
Edinburgh Napier University
February 2010

This book ͏
and early 18th͏
areas but no w͏
innumerable ͏
1745-46 risin͏
of that time a͏
authors alike.͏
some work is͏
Life was ͏
welfare state͏
looked after ͏
above the Hi͏
understandir͏
gillies and c͏
Life in th͏
drank, their ͏
Darien Sche͏
What were ͏
will be high͏
Clan tar͏
will explair͏
wore High͏
Culloden. ͏
every soci͏
of their pu͏
battles fro͏

List of Subscribers

Anthony Carson
John Conn
Marion Conn
Michael Corby
David Cunningham
Na Fir Dileas
Matthew Donnachie
Robert Jensen
Peter MaCaskill
Lachlan MacLean
Alistair MacNeill
Joan Milne
Gordon Nicolson
Jennifer Robertson
Meredith Robertson
Andrew Purden
Colin Rutherford
Maureen Rutherford
Elspeth Spouse
Stacey Whyte

For the Ladies and Gentlemen who subscribed to this book and believed in what I was doing I give my resounding gratitude.

Acknowledgements

I would like to thank Barbara Whyte for her patience and understanding whilst I spent many an hour behind a computer writing or conducting my research. Nostalgia obliges me to thank my uncle Allan Robertson with his intriguing story of apprehension by police regarding the disappearance of the Stone of Destiny. The authorities actually thought he had something to do with the disappearance of the Great Stone. Allan my mother Joan and my father Charles Milne gave me an insatiable appetite for Scottish history. Thanks must be given also to the late Nigel Tranter who listened, with patience to my inquisitive queries regretfully; I did not meet him enough times to be a total nuisance.

Thanks are extended to the National Trust of Scotland, The Circle of Gentlemen, Pat and Steven Davis from Culloden House Hotel for their kind hospitality over the years. I would also like to thank Sean Findlay, Jude Coles, Ian Shields, Gillian and Michael Markey and Paul Clark and Kenneth Campbell from The Carson Clark Gallery in Edinburgh.

Special thanks are extended to Gordon Nicolson Kiltmakers in Edinburgh, and Professor Frank McManus of Edinburgh Napier University, John Lloyd, editor and journalist for his enduring inspiration. Special thanks are also given to Mathew Donnachie for the donation of the 18th century piece of tartan which is illustrated on the front cover, Michael Corby for the donation of the early 19th century doublet. Finally, special thanks are due to John Barnett for his fine weaponry illustrations and also Fred and his son Anthony Carson for their help with the fine portrait of a Highland Gentleman.

Introduction

To the normal Lowland Scot or Englishman, the Highlands were believed to be inexplicable and full of feral kinfolk. Therefore, the majority of people at that time had nothing but contempt for those above the highland line. It was not until after General Wade built the military roads in the Highlands (1725-1736) that a little understanding of Highland culture, traditions and highland dress was obtained. Men of letters had traveled into the depths of the Highlands[1] previously to the roads being built but there were no maps that could be properly relied on. Therefore, the moors, rivers, bogs and rugged terrain for the vast majority were unknown boundaries. Apart from the geological boundaries there was also the language barrier. The common tongue above the highland line was Gaelic. With few exceptions that were able to speak English. Anyone who could not speak Gaelic was undoubtedly viewed with antagonism. The Lowland Scots and English also regarded those above the line as illiterate. The majority were and this state of affairs continued for some time after Culloden in 1746. Burt, who helped build the roads for Wade wrote that there was a common saying in the Lowlands "show me a Highlander, and I will show you a Thief". Burt was one of the few men who visited the Highlands with an impartial view. He spent nearly eleven years in the Highlands and because of his unbiased account he did not agree with that aphorism. Johnston also made a noteworthy comment nearly fifty years later after he visited the Western Highlands in 1773 "I am always sorry when any language is lost, because languages are the pedigree of nations"[2].

Written records were few and far between in the Highlands. The clan chief was the law amongst his clan and oral communication gave cognizance which was better favoured than mere pieces of paper amongst the Highlanders, mainly the common clansmen. The trust and

---

[1] M Martin *A Description of the Western Islands of Scotland Circa 1695* (1703, p 4-5) was a native from Skye who travelled to the Lowlands frequently. Martin was a Gaelic speaker who graduated from Edinburgh University with an MA. He later studied at Leydon for his MD to become a doctor.

[2] Samuel Johnson *A journey to the Western Islands of Scotland* (1773, p 13)

loyalty amongst the Highlanders could not possibly be perceived in the Lowlands of Scotland and England either. Resentment for folk south of the highland line was enforced through the Government by oaths of allegiance i.e., the massacre of Glencoe, the Darien scheme, the Treaty of Union, the Disarming Acts, tax laws and other restrictive trading laws. The old Highland way of life finally came to an end after the battle of Culloden on 16th April 1746. The old clan system was extinguished and Scotland was changed forever, but a new breed of Scots finally emerged after the Highland clearances.

There are innumerable books on the subject of Bonnie Prince Charlie and the 1745-46 rising. This is understandable due to the charismatic figures of the time and it is only right that they have demanded attention from authors alike. In making that statement it has to be emphasized that some work is just clearly romantic fiction based on some facts. Therefore, the late 17th and early 18th centuries are therefore open to further ingenious, inquisitive study.

This book is intended to elucidate certain aspects of this period with some chronology thrown in. Certain references are made to characters out with the perimeters of the book. I must also mention that some parts have been written with dogmatic humour mainly for my own amusement therefore, no insults are intended. I have also tried to be impartial but historical truth will always have discrepancy depending on the writer. For readers with better knowledge, time and resources I give my apologies for any errors made. My aspirations are to be an intellectual hooligan although I realise I will never succeed in comparison to the likes of Ian Hamilton QC, another inspirational character.

Fere libenter hominess id quod volunt credunt
Men willingly believe what they wish
Julius Caesar

Photograph of original map by Hoffman circa 1715
Kindly supplied by Carson Clark Gallery Edinburgh

Contents

The targe
Scottish powder horns
Highland pistols

Appendix 5 p149

General list of makers marks on Scottish blades imported from Solingen.

List of illustrations

Bibliography p151

Authors Biography p162

Index p163

Chapter I

The clan chief and his clansmen

P rior to the battle of Culloden fought on 16th April 1746 the
Highlands of Scotland were divided geographically by the clan
system. The word clan or *clanna* in Gaelic simply means
children therefore, through the clan system everyone was related to
one another within their clan, admittedly to a degree. A clan consisted
of people with the same surname often with attached septs. A sept was
a smaller branch of people who were attached to the clan normally
with a different surname. This meant that the clan as a whole gave the
premise of an extended family. In many cases a family would adopt
the clans surname making them more analogous. The amount of
fighting men within a clan dictated the clans' strength.

The chief of a clan held his position through his pedigree, the
feudal system, and old Celtic traditions (*ipso facto*). The chief and
chieftain's[3] who held a territorial title did not look down on their
clansmen as mere vassals. Likewise the clan members looked up at
their chief or chieftain more as a father figure. Through the inherited
culture and traditions the chief and chieftains had absolute power over
their clansmen and affiliated or adopted septs. Unfortunately, this also
meant the chief could highly influence which King his clansmen
obeyed and what religion they should profess. The trust and loyalty of
the clansmen was generally without question, believing the chief acted
in the whole clans best interests. In contrast when Lord Lovat the
Chief of the Frasers was given a pardon for rape he went over to the
Hanoverian side, his clan immediately deserted him[4].

Clan feuds were common in the 16th and 17th centuries especially
over land which meant every clan would tenaciously hold onto their
property through their feudal inheritance and family connections. This
feudal system meant that fathers passed on from their fathers the same

---

[3] Sir Thomas Innes of Learney Lord Lyon King of Arms *The Tartans of the Clans of Scotland* (1964, p 32)
[4] Samuel Johnson *A journey to the Western Islands of Scotland* (1773, p 13)

piece of land for many generations. Large estates were normally leased to Tacksmen who were directly related to the chief. The Tacksmen would in turn sub-divide the land to the clansmen who would then pay him rent largely in kind. This payment would take the form of food in one form or another. If there were no spare provisions within the family then perhaps labour of some kind would suffice.

An estate that brought in £300 yearly would have approximately £40 paid in coin[5]. During extremely hard times the clan chief would have these reserves that he would pass out amongst the clan as Martin noted amongst Macneil of Barra's Clan[6.] If a member of the clan became ill or unable to look after themselves then they would also be looked after regardless of age.

The Clan Chief and his Gillie's

When a highland chief travelled from his glen he would be accompanied by an entourage of attendants or gillies as they were commonly known in the Highlands. They all played an important role to their chief. One of the gillies present would be his Henchman who was basically his main bodyguard, in truth all clansmen were their chief's or chieftain's bodyguard[7]. One of the Henchman's duties was to stand behind his chief at the dining table and listen quietly to the conversation of those in the vicinity ensuring that his chief was not insulted in any way. Burt gave a short narrative of one youthful gilli who did not understand one word of English[8]. An English officer was in the company of a highland chief and other fine gentlemen, or as they were known in the Highlands *Duine-Uasals*.

The company had been drinking *ufky* (usky or whisky)[9] and the young Henchman thought an insult had been thrown at his chief. He

[5] G H Graham *The Social Life of Scotland in the Eighteenth Century* (1928, p 162)

[6] M Martin *A Description of the Western Islands of Scotland Circa 1695* (1703, p 68)

[7] M Martin *ibid* (1703, p 52) refers to these men as *lucht-taeh* when the chief was travelling

[8] Edward Burt *Letters from a Gentleman in the North of Scotland to His Friend in London* Volume 2 (1754, p 156)

[9] Edward Burt (1754, p 223) *ibid* Volume 2 this is not a misprint the quote is taken directly from Burt's letters. Eighteenth century writers often wrote an f instead of an s, this normally happens in the middle of a word.

immediately drew his pistol pointed it at the officers' head and then pulled the trigger. Fortunately for the officer the pistol mis-fired he was very lucky to be left unscathed. Martin's observation also noted that the henchmen would guard the chief or chieftain both night and day; he referred to this position as a *galloglach*[10]. This is the kind of loyalty a clan chief had from his clansmen.

The common tongue above the highland line was Gaelic. Only the nobility and prolific gentlemen were able to speak English amongst other languages. To a Highlander anyone who could not speak Gaelic was probably viewed with suspicion and a certain amount of antagonism. Written records were few and far between in the Highlands. Nevertheless, oral communication gave cognizance which was better favored than mere pieces of paper and a man's word was his bond.

The chief would have his spokesman present who had the title of the *Bladier*[11]. He would no-doubt be a gentleman and an educated man. Another man of letters would be the chiefs *Bard* or poet who would have extensive genealogical knowledge of the clan.

One of the *Bards* duties was to obviously record, compose and sing of the great battles fought and of course the prowess of his chief and other members of the clan on the field of battle. One famous poet was Colonel John Roy Stuart (1700-175?)[12]. John Roy came over from France to join Prince Charlie on 31st August 1745. He was given the command of a regiment raised in Edinburgh and served with distinction throughout the following campaigns. However, just before Culloden he had a serious quarrel with Lord George Murray whom he mocked in verse amongst other clans. Roy Stuart shared with Robertson of Struan and Hamilton of Bangour the honour of being a poet for the Prince's cause. One of Stuart's poems translated from his native tongue (Gaelic) reads"[13].

Though Campbells come in thousands

---

[10] M Martin *A Description of the Western Islands of Scotland Circa 1695* (1703, p 52)
[11] Edward Burt *Letters from a Gentleman in the North of Scotland to His Friend in London* Volume 2 (1754, p 158)
[12] N MacGregor *John Roy Stuart: Jacobite Bard of Strathspey* (1998, p84)
[13] A Tayler & H Tayler *Jacobite Letters to Lord Pitsligo 1745-1746* (1930, p 55)

We will not be afraid

It was ironic that Roy Stuart should compose a poem with reference to the Campbells (Campbell in Gaelic is *Caimbeul* which translates in English as crooked mouth)[14]. As well as a poet Roy Stuart was also famed for his swordsmanship and piping. After the battle of Culloden he was in hiding for many months in Glenmore. During this time he also had a number of encounters with the redcoats (Hanoverians) and he later made his escape back to France aboard the *L'Heureux* or the *Le Prince de Conti* where he resumed his position as a Jacobite agent.

Cheape also gives insight from the same period concerning the plaid from the bard Alexander MacDonald who wrote in the 1740s[15].

Bfhearr lean breacan uallach
Mu m ghuaillibh s a char fo m àchlais
Na ge do gheibhinn cota
De n chlo as fearr thig a Sasann

Better for me is the proud plaid
Around my shoulder and put under my arm,
Better than though I would get a coat
Of the best cloth that comes from England

Many other verses have been composed in the past regarding highland dress, arguably none as poignant as Alexander's. Verses were composed by the bards about love stories, drinking bouts and any other memorable reflections of life.

While people south of the Highlands thought of the Highlanders as mere savages they did in fact have a better comprehension of their own history than most other folk below the Highlands. Prebble also mentions that "Lowlanders and English at this time invariably referred to Gaelic as Irish. Although it is an acceptable, if loose, term, in its historical context it was an emotive and pejorative word, betraying a

---

[14] A Mackie *Scottish Pageantry* (1967, p 169)
L A Dunkling *Scottish Christian Names* 2nd edition (1988, p 30)
[15] H Cheape *Tartan* 2nd edition National Museums of Scotland (1995, p 25)

common feeling that the Highlanders were an alien and savage people"[16].

Another gillie was the chiefs *Gilli-Cassue* who would carry him on his back when crossing a river or burn if there was no convenient bridge, which were few and far between. One strong and handsome Scot by the name of Milne became quite famous after carrying King Charles II ashore when he arrived from Holland. From that time onwards the Gillie was known as King Milne[17]. The *Gilli-Comstraine* was another servant who would lead his chief who was mounted on his horse over dangerous mountain regions.

The *Gilli-Trushanarish* would be responsible for his chiefs' baggage.

The *Gilli-More* would carry his chiefs' sword, target and firearms which would without a doubt be a huge responsibility and honour. This is probably where the surname Gillmore derived from.

Lastly, the chief would have his piper who would also be a gentleman in his own right. The piper would have his own gilli who would carry and look after his bagpipes. The famous painting of the Grant piper painted in 1714 by Richard Waitt gives an excellent example of the Highland bagpipes used in the early 18th century. These pipes would have the large base drone but the two tenor drones protrude from the same forked stock tied into the bag[18]. He must have been a very important and respected man to be adorned with such clothing and silver trappings.

Other Highlanders with a variety of skills would follow their chief as part of the entourage. Of course other gentlemen of various professions and fine standing would have their own Gillis's at their disposal. Some clan chiefs may have their gillis in modern day society. However, I doubt a modern day chief or chieftain would have anywhere near the influence compared to a chief or chieftain in the olden days.

---

[16] J Prebble *The Lion in the North* (1981, p 298)
[17] A Tayler & H Tayler *Jacobite Letters to Lord Pitsligo 1745-1746*. (1930, p 63)
[18] James Drummond & Joseph Anderson *Ancient Scottish Weapons* (1881, Plate XLVII) this plate illustrates a beautiful set of carved pipes with the two drones protruding from the one forked stock.

Scottish heraldry

Scots heraldry has been an integral part of the clan system since medieval times and still is. The clan chief's coat of arms and clan crest are the chiefs own property, that is heritable property[19.] Ornamentation using the coat of arms or crest was carried out by clan chiefs and other armiger's gentlemen as illustrated by Cameron of Lochiels snuff-mull dated 1740[20]. Pollard & Oliver also discovered a vast amount of buttons through metal detecting on the battle site of Killicrankie, "many of these were plain, but some carried ornate crests and other designs"[21].

MacDonald of Clanranald cap badge. The crest is a castle with three towers, and an armoured hand with a sword issuing from the centre.
The motto is, My Hope Is Constant In Thee.

Cap badges and other identifiable clan emblems were not worn by chiefs, chieftains or individual clan members in the 17th and 18th century, that is fact.

In modern day highland dress the wearer is allowed by a clan chief to wear a cap badge or any other kind of accoutrement that includes the belt and buckle (garter) with the clan crest in the middle. The clan chiefs' motto is normally written in Latin on the belt. It must be emphasized that this is not the users crest and motto it is the chief of

---

[19] Sir Thomas Innes of Learney Lord Lyon King of Arms *Scots Heraldry* (1956, p 180)
[20] Gordon Foster The National Trust for Scotland *Culloden The Swords and the Sorrows* (1996, p 80, plate 7:7)
[21] Dr. Tony Pollard & Neil Oliver *Two Men in a Trench II, Uncovering the secrets of British Battlefields* (2003, p 231)

the relevant clans' property only. All the wearer is achieving in wearing the badge is to show allegiance to the chief of whom the crest and motto belongs to. The Chief of the clan has three feathers on top of the badge for indication of his status.

Another important aspect regarding Heraldry is that the Lord Lyon King of Arms has sole discretion on all Heraldic matters and even the crown cannot interfere[22]. Heraldry is and always has been an important social aspect throughout the clan system. It should be further pointed out that there need not be any clan connection to signify clan allegiance either; after all, arguably we are all Jock Tamsons' bairns. Any individual may buy any tartan of any description however, there may be limitations to where they can buy it but that is modern day commercialism.

---

[22] Sir Thomas Innes of Learney Lord Lyon King of Arms *Scots Heraldry* (1956, p 110-16)

Sketch of Highlanders at Inverness from
*Letters from a Gentleman in the North of Scotland
to his Friend in London* Volume 1 (1754)

Chapter II

Life in the Highlands

The young Highlander

Male children would start swordplay at an early age; the boys would start to play with sticks at sword fighting. Later on their father's would introduce them on how to use a sword, target, dirk and pistol or musket if he possessed one. This was an important part of growing up for any youth for his self-preservation in a rough country where clans were often at dispute with each other. Therefore, discipline in all these weapons would be important to their training on how to kill an enemy quickly and effectively and of course, how to injure an opponent without causing serious injury[23]. In many cases losing a limb or even death was not the direct result of the injury itself. Death in most cases through injury was a direct result of malpractice or infection. With this in mind most Highlanders were brought up to be even-tempered and offending anyone was the last thing they would want to do.

Clan chiefs would often foster out their oldest son to another clan member's family who was obviously in high esteem[24]. At the age of sixteen or even fourteen a boy would be treated as an adult and be able to fight for his clan. The Chief of the MacLeod clan has a tradition when his son comes of age. His heir has to drink a full horn of claret in one draught. Rory Mors horn is adorned with silver and it holds one and two thirds of a bottle of wine. The tradition goes back to the early sixteen hundreds when Rory was Chief of the clan and it is still carried on to this day. Incidentally the average lifespan in 1700 was around twenty five years; many did live longer mainly due to good nutrition and a conscientious lifestyle. This was noted by Martin when he visited the Western Islands in 1695.

---

[23] W H Murray *Rob Roy MacGregor His life and Times* (1982, p 47)
[24] R D Lobban *The Clansmen* (1969, p 44)

Work in the Highlands

For the majority of Scot's in the Highlands life was hard. Work would start at daybreak and finish when there was no natural light to work by. The work for the majority would be in the fields tendering crops and livestock. Children as well as adults would collect wood for the fire, repair damaged clothing and various other essential tasks. After the Union of 1707 many Lowland gentlemen lost their fortunes and there are many accounts of their sons going into an apprenticeship. Some of these gentlemen themselves became innkeepers or merchants in places like Stirling, Glasgow or Edinburgh. Officers from the Hanoverian army were astonished one time when, visiting a hostelry the innkeeper could hold a conversation in Latin. Highland gentlemen would through poverty become a tacksman, buy a small farm or become an innkeeper. A gentleman of Highland birth would not demean himself to become a shopkeeper if he could help it[25]. This was just the way they were brought up. Yet he would fill tankards and listen to drunken conversations with unperturbed condescension. A Tradesman around the 1700s would only receive 6d a day from his employer and even then most of that remuneration would be in kind. Fourteen incorporated trades were registered in Edinburgh with shoemakers second in wealth to Goldsmiths[26].

Education in Scotland

The educational position in Scotland is eminently high in comparison to preceding epochs. After the reformation there was a lot more emphasis on education in the Lowlands although this was through the church, with more religious teaching. In the 18th century there was a distinct lack of schools in both Lowlands and the Highlands. Schooling would start at the age of five or seven. Children who were fortunate enough to be able to attend school usually had to trudge miles over hill and bog land to attend. Inescapably for all children there would always be something needing done regarding the croft, or in the fields. Above the highland line there was also

[25] H G Graham *The Social Life of Scotland in the Eighteenth Century* (1928, p 35)
[26] R T Skinner *The Royal Mile* (1947, p 76)

superstition, ignorance to a degree and the warlike attitude that many highlanders hereditarily possessed. Apart from these debilitating factors the vast majority of folk just could not afford to send their children to school.

Roads were few and far between even after General Wade built the roads into the Highlands. If they were lucky there may have been tracks that the school children could follow. School work started at seven in the morning despite the weather or seasonal discomforts. Schools were often nothing more than dilapidated huts. Graham mentions that in one school the "roof was so bad that the scholars could not stay because of the rain, the Kirk-Session [ordered] every scholar to bring some straw to thatch the school; but the straw was so scares that the parents could not supply it to their children; therefore only half of the school could be covered"[27]. In some regions there may be a generous laird where a barn, an unused granary or even a vault which was utilized as a schoolroom. Schoolmasters were also relatively poor themselves earning no more than tradesmen of the time.

St Andrews University the oldest in Scotland was founded in 1412 by Henry Wardlaw the Bishop of St Andrews[28]. With the re-establishment of Presbyterianism Professors in Scotland were to swear an oath of allegiance (a confession of faith) to William and Mary. The obvious result was that many great minds of the time did not take the oath and as Graham states there was a stagnation of all intellectual life from 1690 till 1725[29]. Nonetheless great men did augment from a University education, one of those being John Graham of Claverhouse. To study law or medicine students would have to be enthusiastic enough to travel and live in France or Holland for a term of three years. It was not until the 1720s that Scotland could provide any adequate education on these two subjects.

Another form of education of the time was where a clan chief or gentlemen would send their progeny to Aberdeen, Edinburgh or Glasgow to further their education in the art of defense. Fencing was taught by Fencing Masters John Merser in 1663 and Alexander

---

[27] H G Graham *The Social Life of Scotland in the Eighteenth Century* (1928, p 425)
[28] R Mackie *A Short History of Scotland* (1947, p 158)
[29] H G Graham *ibid* (1928, p 499)

McGregor Professor of the Art of Defense in 1733[30]. Manuals on fencing were also available by Sir William Hope (1660-1724) who studied the art of the sword for nearly fifty years. Donald McBane (1664-1730) was another author on the subject who fought for the Hanoverian side at Killicrankie.

Music in the Highlands

Music was another important part of highland life, and still is. The legendary MaCrimmons of Skye, who were hereditary pipers to the Laird of MacLeod, had their college of piping at Dunvegan for over 300 years. Johnson referred to the MaCrimmons and the Rankin's who also had a college of piping in Mull[31], the Rankin's were hereditary pipers to the MacLean's of Mull, Coll, and Duart. Those that had a musical aptitude for the pipes were sent to a college of piping by their chief. Only the best pipers were chosen by the Colleges and their apprenticeship would last for seven years, during which time they would learn to play *piobaireach* (classical music). One of the most famous pipers from the MacCrimmon College was Patrick Og MacCrimmon (1645-1730) who was in Macleods' service in 1685[32].

Other musical instruments used in the Highlands were the violin and harp, the latter more by the nobility and of more antiquity. "Almost any form of music could be used for dancing. The fiddle was the dominant dance-music instrument in the eighteenth century, for dancing-masters traditionally played it to accompany their lessons[33]. If a fiddle was not available its place could be taken by the bagpipe in the Lowlands of Scotland. One of the earliest violin makers on the North East coast of Aberdeen was Robert Duncan. The oldest of his violins that has survived has the year 1742 written on the label inside the instrument. It is also worth noting that a manuscript dated to 1715 also

---

[30] C E Whitelaw *Scottish Arms Makers A biographical dictionary of makers of firearms, edged weapons and armour working in Scotland from the 15th Century to 1870* (1977, p 126-127)

[31] Samuel Johnson *A journey to the Western Islands of Scotland* (1773, p 156)

[32] A K Campsie *The MacCrimmon Legend* (1980, p 56)

[33] David Johnson *Music and Society in Lowland Scotland in the Eighteenth Century* Oxford University Press (1972 pp. 24-25)

from Aberdeen has instructions for tuning the violin strings G, D, A and E. Without doubt violins from Italy, France, Germany and England would be brought in to Scotland. Some well known makers from England included Richard Duke, Nathaniel Cross, Barak Norman and John Barrett[34]. Neil Gow (1727-1807) was probably the most prolific Scottish violinist during the eighteenth century. Another form of music for the Highlanders was *puirt-a-beul* which is the Gaelic for mouth music, this was a repetitive rhythm of humming that was not to dissimilar to the pipes[35].

The use of snuff

In the 17th and 18th century snuff was an integral part of everyday life. Snuff was used by both sexes and by all classes of people. Brook mentions that "The Scot's were so noted a race of snuff takers that after the [risings] of 1715 and 1745 had drawn attention to their manners and customs, the figure of a Highlander became the popular sign for a snuff shop"[36]. The most common material used for a snuff-mull was a ram's horn; other materials used were ivory, pewter, brass and silver. The fittings were often made from pewter, brass or silver. In many surviving examples the lid was engraved with the owners' initials and sometimes a date on a small plaque. Designs of the snuff-mull varied; the most common style was made from the tip of a ram's horn curling in towards the tip. One curious and beautiful example is in the Wallace book, *Scottish sword and dirks* (1970). This snuff-mull is in the form of a carved Highlander, made from ivory and dated to around 1715[37]. This would not be a common Highlanders snuff-mull but a Gentleman of great standing. Some of the larger snuff-mulls would have a small mill for grinding the snuff as mentioned by Foster[38]. Johnson also mentioned on his travels that "snuff is the

---

[34] W Sandys & S A Forster *History of the Violin* (2006, p 262-263)
[35] W H Murray *Rob Roy MacGregor His life and Times* (1982, p 12)
[36] J MacLehose *Scottish History & Life* (Brook, 1902, p 251)
[37] John Wallace *Scottish Swords and Dirks An illustrated reference guide to Scottish edged weapons* (1970, p 2)
[38] Gordon Foster The National Trust for Scotland *Culloden The Swords and the Sorrows* (1996, p 79)

luxury of the highland cottage"[39]. The offering off a pinch of snuff during the early 17th & 18th century was a very similar greeting to how one would shake hands on meeting someone today. If there was any indication of hostility then the appropriate palm of the hand would be presumably attached to a weapon.

Oaths and pledges in the Highlands

Since written records were uncommon above the highland line clansmen would bind an agreement by wetting the ball of their thumbs with their mouth then shake hands. This was considered to be more binding than just giving your word. In more serious situations they would swear an oath and bind it by kissing the blade of their dirk[40]. The Cameron's (Cameron in Gaelic is *Camshron*, meaning crooked nose)[41] swore an oath in this manner never to inform on anyone thieving cattle for a reward. The reward normally money was known as *tascal money* and was regarded as an abhorrent act of treachery. It was probably detrimental to every clan member as a cattle thieving was ubiquitous in the Highlands and even down to the Lowlands. This was very serious business indeed and to transgress this type of oath meant serious consequences. If they were caught breaking this type of pledge the culprit would be stabbed by the same weapon they swore the oath on. Depending on the nature of the oath broken, the person was never seen again. It must be said that oaths of this nature were rarely broken as most Highlanders believed it would also damn their sole to the devil[42]. Pledges of allegiance played a central role in defining the relationship between all Scots. The location of where the oath was being taken also appeared to be of utmost importance to Highlanders according to Johnson[43].

---

[39] Samuel Johnson *A journey to the Western Islands of Scotland* (1773, p 57) the old highland way of life was extinguished by this time but some customs obviously still survived.
[40] Edward Burt *Letters from a Gentleman in the North of Scotland to His Friend in London* Volume 2 (1754, p 244)
[41] A Mackie *Scottish Pageantry* (1967, p 169)
[42] Edward Burt *ibid* Volume 1 (1754, p 250)
[43] Samuel Johnson *ibid* (1773, p 220)

28

Cottages and highland huts

The cottages and huts were not very high (around six feet) and similar in construction to stone dykes. There was no chimney, only an aperture near the middle of the hut for the smoke to escape. A fire would be constantly present in the middle of the cottage on a hearth-stone forever giving off the reek of burning peat. The thatching was made from ferns or heather tied with ropes made from heather or straw, straw being mostly used to feed the cattle. The thatch in turn would be held down by weighted stones. The cottages and huts were normally divided into two compartments with the family at one side and their live stock in the other. Bedding would simply consist of hay with the plaid thrown over for expediency. With the fresh air and abundance of space above the Highland line sanitation was far better compared to the Lowland towns. However, Lowland towns were likely to have more community involvement when it came to agriculture. On the other hand the rural districts in the Lowlands would have the same sanitation as the Highlands.

In most cottages or huts there would normally be one large drinking vessel made from wood, horn or pewter that would be passed around the family or guests. Spoons again were made from wood, horn or pewter and were the only eating utensils along with a few knives in some households. Whisky or brandy would be passed around amongst the group of friends in a *Cap* or *Coif*[44] or what is commonly known now as a quaich. The quaich is a round bowl with two or three lugs at the top for holding. In some examples the quaich was made from different coloured staves of wood for example, ebony and boxwood adorned with silver. Stuart mentions that in some Edinburgh taverns the Jacobites and Episcopal clergy toasted to the King over the water drinking from "the wooden quaichs or *caups*"[45]. Quaich's, in general were highland in manufacture and probably made by the local craftsmen. Many of these vessels were rather shallow and it was a common sight to see the draught of brandy or *usky* blown into the

---

[44] Edward Burt *Letters from a Gentleman in the North of Scotland to His Friend in London* Volume 1 (1754, p 188)
[45] M W Stuart *Old Edinburgh Taverns* (1952, p 94)

drinkers face with the wind[46]. If no quaich was available then a sea shell would suffice[47] probably a clam shell although no further description is given.

Diet of the Highlanders

The main diet was broth made from kail (cabbage) and various vegetables also barley, porridge and oatcakes which the Highlanders called bread. Eggs, and butter with cheese were also a common part of the highland diet with mutton on certain occasions. Goats' milk, sheep's milk (which is always boiled first)[48] and ale were the common drink for most folk. Highlanders near the coast would have fish and all kinds of shellfish giving those Highlanders a healthier diet. During summer beef, mutton and fish would be salted for preservation for the lean months of winter and export to other countries. Martin mentioned that in the Isle of Harris beef was salted and preserved in the animals hide[49]. Duck, venison, beef, rabbits and fish would not be as common as one would think. Wheat was produced in the Lowlands and when a farmer in 1727 "cultivated eight acres of wheat in Aberdeenshire it was considered so remarkable that the whole neighborhood was excited"[50]. In truth, the Highlanders were fairly reluctant to changes of any description unless it was already familiar to them. Potatoes and turnips were introduced into the Lowlands around the 1720s with only a few proprietors planting any seed. It was not until the late 1740s that the potato was cultivated properly in Scotland.

17th and 18th century Medicine

Medical knowledge was sparse to say the least. Guest states that "although medicine had made progress by the [late] 17th century, it

[46] Edward Burt *Letters from a Gentleman in the North of Scotland to His Friend in London* Volume 1 (1754, p 188)
[47] S Johnson & J Boswell *A journey to the Western Islands of Scotland* and *Journal of a tour to the Hebrides with Samuel Johnston* (1974, p 354)
[48] Samuel Johnson *A journey to the Western Islands of Scotland* (1773, p 74)
[49] M Martin *A Description of the Western Islands of Scotland 1695* (1703, p 52)
[50] H G Graham *The Social Life of Scotland in the Eighteenth Century* (1928, p 173)

still had a long way to go as King William III could rely on the very best of medical advice, including the liberal application of powdered crab's eyes to his boils"[51]. Common remedies consisted of herbs, frogs, crushed earthworms and slaters (woodlice) taken orally to name a few[52].

Economics

Bartering was the main method in which rent and all other exchanges of produce or labour was made, as money was scarce. Even as late as 1773 Johnson mentions that in St Kilda bartering was the mode of exchange for goods and labour as money was not yet known[53] although this may be rather hard to believe there is probably an element of truth in what he said. St Kilda is the remotest part the British Isles and in the late 17th century there was probably no more than a few hundred folk who inhabited the island.

The strength of a clan was also measured by the amount of livestock they possessed. Cattle in those days were black or brown in colour and they were smaller compared to the reddish brown cattle one associates with the Highlands now. The MacGregor clan who were situated near the Lowlands obtained bad repute from cattle thieving. This was rife throughout the Highlands. In the Highlands stealing cattle from another clan was an acceptable part of life. However, it did create a lot of clan warfare when it was done on a large scale. Thieving cattle was not acceptable in the Lowlands[54] under any circumstances.

Religion

Sunday was a day for religion and everyone would go to church in their best attire, irrespective of their religion, it was compulsory. Authority by the church over social morals made nearly everything an offence. Even the taking of snuff during a sermon entailed a fine of up

---

[51] K & D Guest *British Battles* (1996, p 179)
[52] H G Graham *The Social Life of Scotland in the Eighteenth Century* (1928, p 50-51)
[53] Samuel Johnson *A journey to the Western Islands of Scotland* (1773, p 170)
[54] W H Murray *Rob Roy MacGregor His life and Times* (1982, p 6)

to 20 shillings[55], a lot of money at that time. Solemn preparations were therefore carried out on the Saturday, for example shaving ones beard and the preparation of food to name a few. It was also a common sight to see the women hobble up to the church in their only pair of shoes. Many of the women would carry their shoes to when they were in sight of the church; they were just so unaccustomed to wearing shoes. In the early day's there was no seating arrangements for worshipers therefore, some folk brought their own. The Church or Kirk was also in a position to hire out creepies or stools for worshippers to sit on. A strong box with two separate locks and keys were used to hold contributions for the benefit of the poor who had to wear their beggar's badge. The two keys were held by different elders to discourage dishonesty on one person's part. The contents were distributed three or four times a year amongst the poor. Beggar's badges were given out territorially therefore disenabling poor unfortunates exploiting their predicament to other regions. This method of charity worked passably enough for the poor until the Union in 1707. Silver coinage was called in to be re-minted with copper coins not being worth the trouble. The Scot's penny was worth only one twelfth of an English penny, the new coinage introduced made the Scot's old coinage virtually worthless[56]. Fortunately for the poor other methods of collecting funds were practiced by the church. A pledge is often found in old church records often where there was an intention of marriage. It does not carry the same commitment as an oath. Therefore, breaking a pledge did not carry the same serious consequences. Upon the promise of marriage a sum of money would be left with the church. In 1725 John Wright broke his matrimonial promise, he forfeited a crown to the poor and in the same year John Shepheard forfeited his sword for a similar broken pledge[57]. All in all the Church or Kirk obtained approximately half of their revenue from imposed moral fines one way or another. Beggar's managed to exist on

---

[55] J MacLehose *Scottish History & Life* (Graham, 1902, p 229)
[56] H G Graham *The Social Life of Scotland in the Eighteenth Century* (1928, p 237) One Scot's penny = 1/12 of an English penny and a pound would only be equivalent to 1s. 8d.
[57] H G Graham *ibid* (1928, p 243)

the meager charity of others and in saying this donations were from those who had very little to give themselves. Generosity did not just stop with the beggars most folk were more than willing to make contributions for the repair of a bridge, the churches roof or indeed anything that the community as a whole required. Again all these acts of charity were hard for the Lowlander and English to comprehend. The communion service was also a very important and solemn occasion for the community whether Episcopalian or of Presbyterian faith. This became even more popular in the early years of the Protestant Church in Scotland. In Scotland communion tokens were distributed amongst the community from at least the 1640s. It is also likely that some of the tokens were used as a symbol of Covenanter or Jacobite loyalty through a secretive shape or symbol on the token.

Taverns and Alehouses

At night the shops and taverns in Edinburgh would have lamps outside to shine light on the High Street and Canongate. This was achieved by a Royal Charter granted by King James VII in 1688 where power was also given to the Magistrates to obtain the finance for the enterprise from the Burgesses[58]. It is not hard to imagine the Jacobite Highlanders traveling down to Stirling, Glasgow or Edinburgh on business and meeting with their fellow Jacobites in haunts like Jenny Ha's or the White Horse Inn. To this day there is still a pub in the Canongate of Edinburgh near the original site by the name of Jenny Ha's named after the 'guidwife' Janet Hall who ran the tavern. Skinner mentions that Jenny Ha's alehouse was in Callender's Entry and it was noted for its fine claret[59]. Wine in Scotland was normally drunk with no additions the English and French were prone to add sugar in their wine during some festivities[60]. The White Horse Inn another pub in the Canongate was reputedly given its name by Mary Queen of Scots while she stabled one of her horses there. Bonnie Prince Charlie is also connected with the Inn having quartered there during the 1745 rising.

---

[58] Oliver & Boyd Publishers *Edinburgh 1329-1929* (1929, p 172)
[59] R T Skinner *The Royal Mile* (1947, p 84)
[60] M Francisque *The Scottish Language as illustrated Civilisation in Scotland* (1882, p 44)

However, like most establishments of antiquity changes have occurred and it is now known as the White Horse (established in 1742).

Taverns were an important part of rural and town life and were frequented by all types of people, where all manners of business would be conducted. When special goods or services were about to be ordered the preliminary negotiations would be carried out in the local tavern at the customers' expense. Naturally this would take some time. Once the goods or perhaps transcript was ready to be passed over, this would be at the merchants' expense in the tavern depending on their capacity. Stuart mentions that out of all the trades and professions the most notable to frequent the local taverns were the lawyers and Judges[61]. Many a judge would also been seen with a bottle of wine or port at hand to refresh one from the previous night during a trial. Indeed many were of the opinion that they were at their best after suitable inebriation, as Stuart summarized [62].

> *"O'er draughts of wine the beau would moan his love;*
> *O'er draughts of wine the cit his bargain drove;*
> *O'er draughts of wine the writer penned the will;*
> *And legal wisdom counsell'd o'er a gill."*

Despite alcohol acceptance and intoxication the vast majority of folk drank and held their own with a certain amount of dignity and decorum.

Highland hospitality

Highland hospitality has always been arguably unsurpassed. One story informs us about Duncan Forbes of Culloden House (1685-1747) who was Lord President at the time and who was in the process of burying his mother. When the long funeral procession finally arrived at the churchyard it was discovered that the corpse had been left behind, such was the consumption of drink on that somber occasion. In many cases the mourning and drinking went on for days

---

[61] M W Stuart *Old Edinburgh Taverns* (1952, p 19)
[62] M W Stuart *ibid* (1952, p 18)

after the deceased had been buried. As one Laird said on his deathbed "for gods sake give them a hearty drink"[63] obviously after he had passed away.

Another narration told of the extravagant hospitality Forbes provided at Culloden House. The custom of the house was to crack open a coconut that had been filled with champagne or any wine of his guests choice. Burt who visited Forbes at one time mentions that very few ever get the chance to leave sober and those that stay are generally in no condition to leave[64]. To accommodate his inebriated guests Forbes's servant's, waiting patiently, used poles under the guest's chair to carte them off to their beds.

Traditions associated with social drinking in the 18th century meant if there were ten guests at the table then ten toasts would be drunk. On top of this there were toasts to absent friends, the hosts' good health, and numerous others suitable for the company at the time. One common toast was, glasses charged (a slight pause) fine, "May the wind of adversity ne'er blaw open our door"[65] everyone would applaud and then empty their glass. Jacobite toasts were often made to the King over the water James was in exile. When King William died in 1702 a popular Jacobite toast was made to the gentleman in black velvet. William fell of his horse when it stumbled on a mole hill. Toasting at a table or anywhere else for that matter meant emptying your glass. It is worth noting that to not finish the drink would have been far too disrespectful to the host and the other guests. Burt tells us that perseverance was practically a point of honor at Forbes's table[66]. Both ladies and men drank ale or claret in the early part of the eighteenth century. The Union did however bring more importation of goods mostly for the benefit of the wealthy, unless it was smuggled. The consumption of tea became very fashionable in the 1720s amongst ladies and gentlemen who could afford it. One thing may be certain,

---

[63] H G Graham *The Social Life of Scotland in the Eighteenth Century* (1928, p 53)
[64] Edward Burt *Letters from a Gentleman in the North of Scotland to His Friend in London* Volume 1 (1754, p 161)
[65] H G Graham *ibid* (1928, p 78)
[66] Edward Burt *ibid* (1754, p 161)

tea would not be on Duncan Forbes's table, he totally denounced it as did many ministers, doctors and Town Councils at that time[67].

Nostalgically it must have been something else to see or experience, with all the bob-wigged guests around the table dirks at hand cutting the meat. The gillis's, namely the Henchmen, Piper's and the Bards would be there awaiting their orders. The table would be overflowing with salmon, spit roasted pig, beef, grouse, duck, oysters and all manner of exotic imported fruits that we take for granted now. Pork was not very common in the Highlands nevertheless; Duncan Forbes Lawyer, Statesman and for some debatably a patriot, would have had the meat at his table due to his connections and tastes. On top of that the servants would be continually filling ones glass with the finest claret the moment it was empty. This would all be by the heat and glare of the open fire elucidated by candle light with the piper playing the favorite laments of the host and his guests.

Although Duncan Forbes was not a Jacobite he did include amongst his dear friends some Jacobite's including Simon Lord Lovat[68] and John Gordon of Glenbucket[69]. During the 1715 rising Forbes repelled an attack on Culloden House and took a leading part in the capture of Inverness. Once the rising was over he then protested about the harsh and cruel punishments handed out to the prisoners[70]. Forbes was a rhetoric man but was ridiculed by Cumberland for his compassion for the Jacobites after the 1746 battle on Culloden Moor[71]. He did not believe that repression of Highland culture and traditions would bring peace. He was of belief that change would be better brought about by economic development. All in all Duncan Forbes of Culloden was a rare man of his time. He was undoubtedly a humanitarian who could have changed the course of Scottish history if he had the inclination. Murray mentioned that Forbes saved the Union in 1707[72] and Robertson stated that "Forbes of Culloden was doing all he could to

[67] J MacLehose *Scottish History & Life* (Graham, 1902, p 258) tea costing 30 shillings a pound around this time
[68] W C Mackenzie *Lovat of the Forty-five* (1934, p 161)
[69] A Tayler & H Tayler *Jacobite Letters to Lord Pitsligo 1745-1746* (1930, p 99)
[70] C D Murray *Duncan Forbes of Culloden* (1936, p 6)
[71] A Tayler & H Tayler *ibid 1745-1746* (1930, p 93) Inform us that through certain letters, Forbes was not present at Culloden during the battle.
[72] C D Murray *ibid* (1936, p 43-44)

restrain any Highland chiefs and their clans from taking up arms for the new King James. Had he not done so it is almost certain the Stuarts would have reigned again"[73]?

Hospitality was even provided by those who could little enough afford it. There were many stragglers roaming around the Highlands with no kin to help them. Men of property even if it was just a cottage or a hut did not mind too much if a straggler tapped on their door for shelter. Martin and Johnson made this observation during their visit to the Western Islands "Wherever there is a house, the stranger finds a welcome"[74]. This was a fundamental part of life for many in the Highlands. Gathering around the peat fire the visitors would provide essential information on what was going on in the next Glen and vice versa. If the owner had enough provisions the visitor would be provided with basic food and beverage. In the Highlands this was not regarded as begging, it was just customary hospitality. Burt mentioned with vacillation that when he and others visited a gentleman in the Highlands the house would always appear to have plenty of food and drink he mentions that "they ransack all their tenants rather than we should think meanly of their Housekeeping"[75]. The consequences of which are many tenants will do with out for a week or so rather than have their Laird embarrassed. More often than not the clansmen probably did contribute depending on their personal circumstances.

Burials, Weddings and christenings were also conducted on a grand scale if Highlander's could afford it; if somebody of distinction was buried then claret was there for all. As well as the ale, claret and brandy, food would also be in abundance on the tables. When a young man was setting up house for his future bride the custom was to visit his neighbours and friends. They in turn would provide him with a cow, a sheep or anything else that would be useful. This custom was called *"Thigging"* and it provided the couple with a rudimentary start in life[76].

---

[73] B Robertson *Jacobite Activities in and around Inverness 1688-1746* (1925, p 6-7)
[74] M Martin *A Description of the Western Islands of Scotland Circa 1695* (1703, p 66) Samuel Johnson   *A journey to the Western Islands of Scotland* (1773, p 151)
[75] Edward Burt *Letters from a Gentleman in the North of Scotland to His Friend in London* Volume 2 (1754, p 201)
[76] Edward Burt *ibid* (1754, p 209)

Chapter III

Highland dress in the late 17th and 18th Century

The belted plaid or *feileadh-mòr*

The most common mode of dress for Highlanders was the belted-plaid or as it was known in the Highlands the *feileadh-mòr* (big wrap) or *breachan* (tartan cloth)[77]. One of the earliest mentions of the plaid is by George Buchan (1581). James Aikman translated the transcript and used it in his work '*History of Scotland*' which was published in 1827.

Documentation of the plaid is also given from Ireland, regarding the Life of Red Hugh O'Donnell written by Lughaidh O'Clery in 1594[78]. Red Hugh and others were probably Hebridean mercenaries from the clans Macdonald and Macleod who went over to Ireland. The plaid was a piece of tartan traditionally made from dyed wool homespun in the cottage or by the local weavers. It was only the men that wore the plaid women wore a similar garment called the *arisad*[79]. The length of a belted plaid could vary depending upon the coarseness of the wool and off course the girth of the individual; generally three to five yards were ample. The weaving looms at this time were around twenty eight inches wide. This meant that the plaid was made from two lengths of material stitched together to give a width of around fifty six inches[80]. Tartan[81] at this time did not have any clan connection as we have nowadays[82] see (Appendix 1). However, indigenous plants or

---

[77] H F McClintock & J T Dunbar *Old Highland Dress and Tartans* (1949, p 37)
[78] H F McClintock & J T Dunbar *ibid* (1949, p 18)
[79] M Martin *A Description of the Western Islands of Scotland Circa 1695* (1703, p 129)
[80] J G MacKay *The Romantic Story of the Highland Garb and the Tartan* (1924, p 99)
[81] H F McClintock & J T Dunbar *ibid* (1949, p 57) "[the word tartan] is from the French word "tiretaine" and originally meant a special kind of cloth"
[82] J T Dunbar *History of Highland Dress* (1979, p 46) W H Murray *Rob Roy MacGregor His life and Times* (1982, p 45)

38

materials used in the dying process may have given the experienced traveler a vague indication of where the tartan was woven and hence where the person came from[83].

Another description of the Highland dress was given by Thomas Morer around 1689; his work was not published until 1702 and again in 1715. This is arguably one of the most comprehensive accounts of Highland dress in the late 17th and the early 18th century. Morer mentions, "They are constant in their habit or way of clothing, pladds are most in use with them, which, tho we English thought inconvenient especially for swordsmen in times of action and in heat of summer, as when we saw 'em; yet they excused themselves on these accounts, that they not only served them for cloaths by day in case of necessity but were palates or beds in the night at such times as they traveled and had not opportunities for better accommodation, and for that reason in campaigns were not unuseful: The Lowlanders add, that being too often men of pray, by this means they cover their booty the better, and carry it off without the owners knowledge. These pladds are about seven or eight yards long differing in fineness according to the abilities or fancy of the wearer. They cover the whole body with 'em from the neck to the knees, excepting the right arm, which they keep constantly at liberty. Many of them have nothing under these garments besides waistcoats and shirts, which descent no lower than the knees, and they so gird 'em about the middle as to give 'em the same length as the linen under 'em, and thereby supply the defect of drawers and breeches. Those who have stockings make 'em generally of the same piece with their pladds, not knit or weaved, but sow'd together, and they tie 'em below the knee with tufted garters. They wear a sort of shooes, which they call brocks, like our pumps, without heels, of a very thin sole. They cover their heads with bonnets or thrum-caps, not unlike those of our servitors, tho' of a better consistence to keep of the

---

[83] M Martin *A Description of the Western Islands of Scotland Circa 1695* (1703, p 129) Dunbar mentions that "Whilst many writers quote Martins statement that it was possible to tell where a man came from by his plaid as evidence of a "clan" tartan system, most authoritative writers consider that he meant no more than he said-designs could be identified with districts." This statement has often been misconstrued that there were also identifiable District tartans.

weather. They are blue, grey, or sad coloured as the purchaser thinks fit."[84]

This account of Highland dress evidently observed that there was a variation in the quality of the plaid and the colours used. There is also a clear distinction to the right arm being free for movement compared to the left. It would be a fair assumption that left-handed Highlanders would wear the plaid in a manner to suit their comfort and dexterity. The linen shirts of this period are obviously long, roughly a few inches short from the knee. The shirt being long would provide extra protection from the cold weather. The fact that Morer notes many of them wore little but their shirt and waistcoat under their plaid would make sense during summer, the time he made his observation. Morer also mentions that the English thought the plaid to be awkward in fighting situations. However, he shows rectitude in stating that they excused themselves on these accounts. He is probably referring to the battle of Killicrankie fought in 1689 where some of the Highlanders discarded their plaids before they charged at the enemy[85]. This is secondary information as Morer was not present at Killicrankie; in fact he was quartered in Edinburgh during the Battle[86]. The front ranks of the Jacobite army would be those with the best weapons, clan chiefs and gentlemen of standing who possessed muskets, pistols and of course a sword and Target. It is fair to assume that it is these gentlemen most of whom wore trews would be the Highlanders likely to discard their upper garment, probably the smaller shoulder plaid. Arguably some clansmen without trews would have done likewise as mentioned by Morer and other contemporary writers. If the Highlanders were victorious in battle then there would be plenty time to gather up garments to wear with the other spoils of war.

---

[84] Rev. Thomas Morer *A Short Account of Scotland.* (1702, p 99) Reprinted London (1715) as "*A Short Account of Scotland, etc*
[85] Edward Burt *Letters from a Gentleman in the North of Scotland to His Friend in London* Volume 2 (1754, p 224)
[86] Rev. Thomas Morer *ibid* (1702, p 99) Morer was the Chaplain to Sir John Lanier's regiment (Queens Dragoons)

Another early description of Highland dress was made by John Macky in 1723[87] his account distinguishes between the Highland gentlemen and their Gilles. Macky who was residing at Stirling visited Crieff Fair, more out of curiosity than anything else. "The Highland gentlemen were mighty civil, dressed in their slash'd short Waistcoats, a Trousing (which is Breeches and Stockings of one piece of strip'd Stuff) with a plaid for a cloak, and a blue Bonnet. They have a Ponyard, Knife and fork in one sheath hanging at one side of their belt, their Pistol at the other, and their Snuff-Mill before; with a great Broadsword by their side. Their Attendance [sic] were very numerous, all in Belted Plaids, girt like Women's Petticoats down to the Knee; their Thighs and half of the lag bare. They had also each their Broadsword and Ponyard"[88]. Macky's description noticeably indicates that the Highland gentlemen wore trews of stripped material[89] presumably tartan and that they wore their plaids as a kind of cloak that could be wrapped around their shoulders. If a gentleman was traveling on horseback then the trews were far more practical. For these gentlemen the plaid was worn bandolier fashion around the body and it would also be used as a blanket when necessary. However, gentlemen did wear the plaid as full dress which was also considered a fashionable costume[90]. Evidence for this can be seen in the various paintings from the 17th and 18th century. It is therefore fair to say that the Highland gentlemen considered the plaid as not just the common dress of their clansmen.

Wearing the plaid

McClintock and Dunbar give an excellent description of the belted plaid and how to wear. "The plaid was a length of tartan cloth, about 5 ft wide, made of two single widths of about 30 inches sewn together

---

[87] John Macky *A Journey Through Scotland* (1729, p 194)

[88] John Macky *ibid* (1729, p 194)

[89] The painting by R Waitt of Donald Grant of Glenbeg dated 1719 illustrates a tartan striped in one direction only as illustrated in H F McClintock & J T Dunbar's *Old Highland Dress and Tartans* (1949, plate 18)

[90] H Cheape *Tartan* 2nd edition National Museums of Scotland (1995, p 14)

A fine oil painting by Artist Fred Carson
of a Highland Piper (Anthony Carson)
wearing the plaid with some Modern accoutrements

normally 12 to 18 feet in length. To use it as a belted plaid the wearer would start by laying it out on the ground and would proceed to fold it neatly in transverse pleats until he had reduced its length to 4 or 5 feet, leaving a foot or more at each end unpleated. He would then lie down on it in such a way that it s lower edge was level with [the back of] his knees and after folding the two unpleated ends across [the front of] his body so that they overlapped, would fasten the whole thing round him with a belt"[91]. He would then stand up and pull the two aprons one at a time arranging and tucking the corner into the back of the plaid under the belt. The remaining part hanging at the back was normally brought up and attached to a button stitched onto the doublet usually the left shoulder. Another way was to use a bodkin of bone or a wooden pin again securing it to the shoulder. The material left hanging at the back would normally be fixed to the shoulder one way or the other[92]. Prince Charlie is reputed to have given Lady Macintosh 'Colonel Anne' a gold pin that he used to secure his plaid to his shoulder[93]. Arguably, silver or gold pins may have been used to secure the plaid by those who could afford them, which would have been very few. I tend to agree with Dunbar and other researchers in the past have made it clear that, there is little doubt left that it was only the women who wore plaid brooches of any description[94]. The wearer of the plaid could also wrap it over one shoulder and the other end could be brought under the other arm crossing over the front of the abdomen and fastening the two ends by a piece of leather thong or again a bone bodkin. Modern day wearers of the plaid tend to wear it in this fashion and there is evidence to suggest this method was used in the 17th and 18th century[95].

---

[91] H F McClintock & J T Dunbar *Old Highland Dress and Tartans* (1949, p 19)
[92] Edward Burt *Letters from a Gentleman in the North of Scotland to His Friend in London* Volume 2 (1754, p 185) Burt mentions a bodkin of bone or sometimes they use a sharpened piece of stick and
M Martin *A Description of the Western Islands of Scotland Circa 1695* (1703, p 60) also made the same observation.
[93] J Paton *Scottish National Memorials* (1896, p 138)
[94] J T Dunbar *History of Highland Dress* (1979, p 220)
[95] H Cheape *Tartan* 2nd edition National Museums of Scotland (1995, p 25) the poem by A MacDonald in Chapter 1 may suggest this.

Some modern day wearers of the plaid tend to wear the garment leaving the excess material hanging at the back. This is slightly obscure if you consider the climate and terrain of the Highlands. The topography of bogs, mountains regions and lack of roads would make it obviously impractical to wear it in this fashion in the 17th and 18th century. The only time a plaid would not be fixed to the shoulder is when it was brought over the head and shoulders for added protection from the weather. The plaid to all Highlanders was versatile and without doubt a necessary piece of clothing especially when away from home for whatever reason. A cross belt obviously carrying a sword would have been worn under the plaid for obvious reasons.

The small kilt or *feileadh-beag*

Evidence is severely lacking as to the exact origins of the kilt and no other Scottish garment has caused more contention amongst scholars alike. No distinction is made by the earlier writers in the late 17th and early 18th century namely Martin and Burt. Nevertheless, one theory relating to the origins of the small kilt comes from a letter originally written in 1768, which had no profile until it was printed in the *Edinburgh Magazine* in 1785. The letter describes how an Englishman by the name of Thomas Rawlinson carried out work in Glengarry and Lochaber fifty or so years before the letter was first written[96]. Rawlinson employed Highlanders in his iron works. He was innovative and had no bias towards highland dress, namely the plaid. He thought it far more convenient for his workers to cut the top portion of the plaid and stitch the lower portion together, thus giving the stitched pleats and the *feileadh-beag*.

Other theories basically have no conclusive evidence to support them. MacKay provides a more descriptive date of 1728 to Rawlinson and various references to heraldic achievements where the supporters on either side of the shield wear the small kilt[97]. MacKay states that the Arms of the Burnetts of Leys who were granted arms in 1626 are authority to the *feileadh-beag* being in use in the 17th century. MacKay

[96] H F McClintock & J T Dunbar *Old Highland Dress and Tartans* (1949, p 46)
[97] J G MacKay *The Romantic Story of the Highland Garb and the Tartan* (1924, p 68-69)

also mentions the arms of Skene[98] matriculated on 1672. Another reference is made to Gordon Rothiemay's map of Aberdeen by MacKay showing a boy in a kilt dated 166. However, McClintock and Dunbar have thrown elucidation on these claims[99].

The authority for using the arms of the Burnetts of Leys is false because the illustration referred to is from a water colour painted in 1899. The carving at Skene House of the arms of Skene are so weathered proper analysis is therefore unobtainable. The depiction of the arms of Skene in Nisbet's Heraldic Plates where actually drawn in the 19th century. Contention also stands regarding the sundial's contemporary accuracy since it was made in 1736 the date of matriculation was actually 1672. There is also a photograph showing the arms of Skene from a drawing of a stone supposedly dating to 1672[100]. McClintock, has the stone dated to 1672 whereas Dunbar has the date set to 1692, most probably a misprint. The sundial and the photograph of the stone are also slightly different regarding the dress of the supporters. Since no direct link can be determined by all three references, each one was subject to differential artistic impression thus making them all unreliable. The map by Rothiemay of Aberdeen was drawn by a Dutch artist and also engraved in Holland. It is more than plausible that it was a Dutch civilian of the time portrayed on the map. Furthermore, maps made during this time were unreliable as mentioned in the Introduction however; map makers of the time were still trying to accurately include all details. If it were a depiction of a Highlander surely the Dutch would have the figure detailed in tartan. What we do know for certain is that by the middle of the 18th century the kilt was commonly worn. In my opinion, it is irrespective whether a Scotsman or an Englishman came up with the idea for the small kilt. It is plain to see that the *feileadh-beag* derived from the *feileadh-mòr*. The facts remain that the *feileadh-beag* was worn in the early 18th

[98] Sir Thomas Innes of Learney Lord Lyon King of Arms *The Tartans of the Clans and Families of Scotland* (1964, p 5) heavily disputes the claims that an "Anglo-Saxon engineer" invented the kilt with reference to the arms of Skene.
Sir Archibald Campbell also referred to the arms of Skene in his defence for the feileadh-beag against Rawlinson in *Highland Dress Arms and Ornament* (1899, p 119-121)
[99] H F McClintock & J T Dunbar *Old Highland Dress and Tartans* (1949, p 42-45)
[100] J T Dunbar *History of Highland Dress* (1979, p 54)

century and is still worn today, with slight changes to the 18th
century pattern. Parliament enforced the Dress Act in 1747 forbidding
Highland dress which included the "plaid, *philabeag* or little kilt,
trowse, shoulder belt" and so forth.

Doublets and waistcoats

In the late part of the 17th and early 18th century the doublet was
made from cloth or velvet and commonly slashed at various parts on
the arms, the abdomen and sometimes the back of the body. This
would allow the contrasting inner material to show through. The
portrait of Lord Duffas (Kenneth Sutherland) painted by Richard Waitt
in 1700 is a good example showing this style of fashionable doublet.
The doublet is crimson with a green lining, not only is this doublet
slashed at various points it is scalloped at the edges. Doublets were
short and cut close to the body. Another method used in slashing was
to let the shirt flow through the openings of inner and outer material.
This style of doublet also gave a lot more freedom of movement,
which arguably the Highlanders would need traversing over the moors
and mountainous regions. Fashions were slow in mode coming into the
Highlands and thus slow to displacement. This was again due to the
financial deficiency of most Highlander's and their slow assimilation
to change. If the material was tartan it was normally cut on the bias
that is cut diagonally to the checked pattern. This allowed more stretch
to the material and therefore a closer fit to the body. The first piece of
pictorial evidence for a tartan doublet is the painting of Major Fraser
of Castle Leather (1670-1750) painted around 1723[101]. The name of
the artist is unknown. Therefore it would be a fair assumption that
tartan doublets came into vogue around the early 1700s.

The waistcoat was usually cut about six inches longer than the
doublet. Doublets and waistcoats would generally have the same
amount of buttons both buttoned up to the neck. Normally buttons
were made from small cylindrical pieces of wood; some buttons were
slightly padded and covered with the same material as the doublet or
waistcoat. Gentlemen of course had the option if they had the finances
to use pewter, brass or silver buttons. Embroidery work often

---

[101] J T Dunbar *The Costume of Scotland* (1984, p39)

embellished the garment and gold or silver button holes were common amongst the gentlemen too. In the late 17th early 18th century there was no collar on either of the garments however; this was not a general fixed rule[102].

Trews and breeches

Trews probably go a lot further back than most folk would imagine. With conviction there was a pair made for King James V in 1538[103]. Tartan trews are not to be compared with the tartan trousers that we often see worn by the military and civilians nowadays. The original trews were cut on the bias and they were made to fit completely over the foot as well. There was a flap of material over the groin area which was buttoned up on either side. They were worn as close to the leg and ankle as possible and in some cases the ankle part of the trews at times had laces. When these were tied tight to the ankle it helped profile the garment to the leg. The trews were normally tied at the top of the calf with a garter similar to the hose. Martin mentions that they were made from coloured material and some were striped[104] (presumably made from tartan).

As mentioned earlier trews were a garment worn by the wealthier Highlanders and gentlemen who could also afford to travel on horseback. Lowland breaches were generally cut just below the knee and tied again with garters or silk depending on the wearers' disposition. When Lowland breaches were worn hose of one kind or another were also worn. Cheape mentions that "The trews were different from other forms of trousers, and Highlanders came to regard them as a mark of distinction between themselves and Lowland Scots"[105]. However, Highlanders did wear both trews and breeches depending on their status.

---

[102] S Maxwell & R Hutchison *Scottish Costume 1550-1850* (1958, p 69)
[103] Maxwell S., Lindsay T B., Blair C., Wallace J., Reid W., Scott J G., Norman A V B., *Scottish Weapons. The Scottish Art Review Magazine* published by the Glasgow Art Gallery and Museums Association. Volume 9 No 1, (1963, p 8)
[104] M Martin *A Description of the Western Islands of Scotland Circa 1695* (1703, p 128)
[105] H Cheape *Tartan* 2nd edition National Museums of Scotland (1995, p 19)

Hose or socks

The Highland hose or socks at this time were normally cut from the cloth either plain coloured or tartan, again this was clearly observed by Morer[106]. Similar to the doublet they were cut on the bias and stitched at the back. Normally the tartan was made from a slightly smaller check to the plaid. Being cut on the bias gave more stretch to the material allowing it to fit neatly to lower part of the leg. The hose were tied to the leg just above the two calf muscles with garters. Gentlemen again, had the option for modifying the hose in a decorative fashion. The portrait earlier referred to of Alastair Grant (1714) depicts the hose with a kind of plumage at the back seem, with grandiose decoration. The portrait of a Highland chieftain (1660?) also has Murray with the hose triangulated at the top of the leg.

The Scottish bonnet

The flat blue or grey bonnet was in use by almost every male in the Lowlands as far back as 1598 however; McClintock states that it was not until later that this type of bonnet was adopted in the Highlands[107]. Martin who was factor to the Laird of Macleod described the Highlander's bonnet as being made from a thick cloth invariably knitted wool and he described the colours of the bonnets as black, grey or blue[108]. Other writers have described the bonnet as only blue in colour;[109] whereas Brown mentions that it was the poorer men in country districts that wore just the blue bonnets[110].

---

[106] Rev. Thomas Morer *A Short Account of Scotland.* (1702, p 99) Reprinted London (1715) as "*A Short Account of Scotland, etc*

[107] H F McClintock & J T Dunbar *Old Highland Dress and Tartans* (1949, p 15)

[108] M Martin *A Description of the Western Islands of Scotland* (1703, p 128)

[109] W Sacheverell *An account of the Isle of Man, with a Voyage to I-Columb-kill* (1702, p 125) described the Highlanders in Mull as having blue bonnets as well as John Macky *A Journey Through Scotland* (1729, p 194)

[110] H Brown *A Short History of Scotland* (1951, p 275)

48

Foot wear

For normal Highlanders footwear would consist of a single piece of thick hide. This would be cut from cow skin, deerskin or even a horse with the hair left on the outside. Leather thronging was used to secure them at the back and another piece of thronging would be used to lace up the front. This type of footwear was commonly known in the Highlands as *cuarans*[111]. Burt refers to this footwear as *"Quarants"* which were often unsightly to the eyes and unpleasant to the nose[112]. This form of footwear was light and supple giving some protection from the rough terrain. This was one of the domestic arts that every Highlander male and female would be taught from early years[113]. The clansmen were able to traverse over long distances compared to others who wore thick-soled shoes or boots[114]. In fact, many of the Highlanders would travel without footwear. Johnson points out that "they [the Highlanders] are accustomed to run upon rough ground, and therefore can with great agility skip over the bog or clamber the mountain"[115]. Chiefs and Highland gentlemen would invariably have soled shoes some with a buckle of brass or silver and they would be more accustomed to wearing them compared to their clansmen.

Sporrans

The earliest form of a sporran was nothing more than a deerskin or calfskin pouch. Thongs would be laced through at the top and tied for closure. Thongs also had tassels added at the end probably more for decoration than function. Sometimes the sporran was made from other material[116] such as cloth however, these are rather rare or they have

---

[111] J G MacKay *The Romantic Story of the Highland Garb and the Tartan* (1924, p 100)
[112] Edward Burt *Letters from a Gentleman in the North of Scotland to His Friend in London* Volume 2 (1754, p 185-186)
[113] Samuel Johnson *A journey to the Western Islands of Scotland* (1773, p 118)
[114] W H Murray *Rob Roy MacGregor His life and Times* (1982, p 39)
[115] Samuel Johnson *ibid* (1773, p 129)
[116] The portrait of Major Fraser of Castle Leather (1670-1750) displays a rather curious example made from cloth in H F McClintock & J T Dunbar *Old Highland Dress and Tartans* (1949, plate 15)

clearly not survived the rigors of time. In the late 17th and early 18th century sporrans were produced with metal clasps commonly of brass manufacture. These would either be a half circle or angular in shape. Intricate engraving was common as well as the pierced heart decoration seen on many sword hilts, dirk pommel caps and target bosses of the era. At the back of the piercings there is normally red material, often velvet to enhance the decoration. There may also be some truth in material from the captured red coats from the Hanoverian army being used for trophies and decoration of this nature. One particular sporran with a brass cantle in Drummond's book[117] has the following engraved on the front of the cantle along with beautiful foliaged scroll work.

"Open my mouth, cut not my skin.
And then you'll see what is Therin"

There is a description of Rob Roy's sporran in Paton's *Scottish National Memorials*[118], which is given here "The strong brass frame at the top is ornamented with a series of concentric rings", it is 5 5/8 inches broad and the depth is 7 7/8 inches. "It has three leather looped tags, with tassels of the same material". Whether or not it was Rob Roy's sporran one will probably never know for certain. In Fitzroy MacLean's' book *Highlanders* there is a picture of what he calls Rob Roy's sporran which more or less corresponds with Paton's description. In contrast, Maclean also states that the picture similar to the Alistair Mohr Grant is an anonymous painting of Rob Roy which is totally erroneous[119].

Some of the locking mechanisms on these sporrans were quite tricky, and sporrans with two separate, different locking mechanisms were not unknown. Interestingly enough, Sir Walter Scott describes Rob's sporran as having a pistol incorporated into the cantle which

---

[117] James Drummond & Joseph Anderson *Ancient Scottish Weapons* (1881, Plate XXXVIII)
[118] J Paton *Scottish National Memorials* (1896, p 126)
[119] F Maclean *Highlanders A History of the Highland Clans* (1995, p 193)

50

would go off if someone attempted to open it without prior knowledge[120].

Sporrans with a brass or silver cantle would without doubt be a status symbol during Jacobite times and only the wealthy could afford to have one made. There would not be any set pattern to a finished sporran either; in other words, one could not just buy a sporran of this type of the shelf. Each one was probably made to the buyers' specifications.

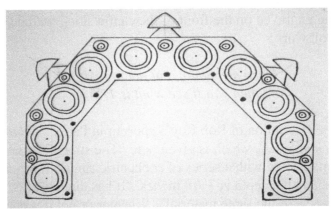

Sketch by Author of Rob Roy's sporran cantle made from brass and taken from F Maclean's *Highlanders A History of the Highland Clans* (1995)

Women's dress

The common dress for women above the highland line was the arisad. This was similar to the man's plaid only shorter in length and finer in quality. The colour of the woman's arisad was commonly white with a few small stripes black, blue and red[121]. Sacheverell wrote "The habit of both sexes is the pladd; the women's much finer, the colours more livelily, and the squares larger than the men's, and

[120] Sir Walter Scott *Rob Roy The Waverly Novels* Dryburgh edition Volume IV (1893, p 341-342)
[121] H F McClintock & J T Dunbar *Old Highland Dress and Tartans* (1949, p 27)

put me in mind of the ancient Picts. This garment serves them for a veil, and covers both head and body"[122]. The garment was tied at the neck with a brooch in such a fashion so that it draped over the shoulders. It was also tied at the waist with a belt with the remainder of material hanging down to the ankles. Similar to the man's plaid it could be brought up over the head for extra protection from the weather. The brooch would be a symbol of the woman's' wealth either made from pewter, brass or silver. Beautiful Celtic engraving is often seen on these functional pieces of jewelry similar to the targes and powder horns worn by Highland gentlemen. Along with the arisad females wore a short petticoat made from wool reaching down to their knees. Women who were married or pregnant out of wedlock (god forbid) generally wore a head cloth or kerchief[123] of red or blue, ordinary girls were bare headed as mentioned by Burt and other writers. Shoes were hardly worn by women at all and if shoes were worn it was for going to Church on a Sunday or, possibly, to a big social event.

The dyeing process of wool

The roots bark and berries used in the wool dyeing process were mostly indigenous and therefore available throughout the Lowlands and Highlands. Black dye could be made from Alder tree bark or dock root. Black dye was expensive to produce therefore only the rich could wear garments made from black dye. Brown dye from stone parmelia or blaeberry with gall nuts and blue dye form blueberry with alum. The wool in raw form was soaked and cleaned in a barrel which contained urine to remove the oils and filth. Once it was cleaned in a stream or river it was then subjected to the dying process (Appendix 3). The clean wool was then soaked or boiled in water with the roots, bark, or powders to extract the colour. The wool was then spun on a spindle and bobbin into yarn and then woven on a loom using a small pattern stick. Waulking the material was the final process; this would thicken the fibers which helped with the waterproofing of the finished

---

[122] W Sacheverell *An account of the Isle of Man, with a Voyage to I-Columb-kill* (1702, p 125)

[123] H Cheape *Tartan* 2nd edition National Museums of Scotland (1995, p 19)

garment. This was mostly all women's work; they would wash the material and then stamp and tumble it with their feet. Labours of this nature were often done with the accompaniment of their traditional mouth music. Some dyes were imported from other countries for example; indigo (a rich blue colour) was imported from Holland regularly to St Kilda[124]. Only the rich could afford to pay for the importation of rich colourful dyes. The clan chief and duine usaels would be the initial beneficiaries from the rich colouring from these dyes. The second batch of goods dyed from the same liquid would obviously have a lighter colour; this would be used for the majority of folk. In early tartans there also appears to be a fair amount of undyed wool in the tartan indicating again the frugal ways for the majority[125]. The following translation from Latin is taken from McClintock's *Old Highland Dress and Tartan*. "They delight in variegated garments, especially stripes, and their favourite colours are purple and blue. Their ancestors wore plaids of many colours, and numbers still retain this custom and the majority now in their dress prefer a dark brown, imitating nearly the leaves of the heather, that when lying upon the heath in the day, they may not be discovered by the appearance of their clothes; in these wrapped rather than covered, they brave the severest storms in the open air, and sometimes lay themselves down to sleep even in the middle of the snow"[126]. The original author was George Buchanan (1506-1582) who wrote in Latin *Rerum Scoticarum Historia* (*A history of Scotland*) in 1581. His account was taken from the western islands but is generally accepted to be about the Highlands as a whole. This arguably indicates that the colours used in dying towards the end of the 16th century were inclined to be more indigenous for the common folk. The later part of the 17th century brings slightly more colour variation possibly due to imported dyes and an enhanced social network. It was not uncommon for the clansmen to rub oil or grease into some of their garments as this gave added protection from the wet weather.

In summary wealth distribution was probably never more prominent in a dress perspective compared to the 17th and 18th century.

---

[124] J T Dunbar *History of Highland Dress* (1979, p 227)
[125] H F McClintock & J T Dunbar *Old Highland Dress and Tartans* (1949, p 77)
[126] H F McClintock & J T Dunbar *ibid* (1949, p 9)

One could look at a person and immediately tell their status. The colours cut and decoration of clothing and the weapons they carried would give a clear indication of an individual's repute. Gentlemen had their resplendent costumes with their renowned Ferrara swords with beautifull basket hilts, functional but also decorative. The ladies had beautifully embroidered garments flowing in the ball room. Clan women had their plaid brooches and other pieces of jewellery. One distinction has to be made between the wealthy and extremely wealthy. Noble women would not wear a plaid brooch; they would wear the fashions of the Lowlands that was derivative from London and Paris and so did many highland gentlemen. There was also no such thing as imitation goods as one has nowadays. True, raw materials were imported some contraband which sold at a discount price. However, the quality of goods could not be imitated in the actual manufacture and finish of the garments all being handmade. The word globalization did not even exist if one considers the fact that very few had been in the Highlands.

Chapter IV

Political aspects in Scotland

The Darien scheme

William Patterson a Dumfriesshire man had a vision which would bring wealth to Scotland. This was the same William Patterson who was the Scottish founder of the Bank of England. Patterson had been in the West Indies and therefore had seen with his own eyes the resources that where available for trade[127]. He believed that he could open up trading colonies that would bring vast fortunes to Scotland. William III and Mary II reigned jointly over Scotland, England and Wales from 1689 until her death of smallpox in 1694. Mary was his cousin and eleven years younger. In 1695 William III gave his Commissioner empowerment to provide endorsement for a new joint trading venture between Scotland and England. An Act was passed by the Scottish Parliament that would open up trading between Africa, the Indies and Scotland[128]. A new company was set up called The Company of Scotland, investment poured in. English traders noticed the huge investment pouring in from Scotland, weighed up their benefits and pulled out of the scheme. Paterson also wanted Scotland to trade with their own colonies namely the Isthmus of Darien or Panama. Scotland would have sole right to their trading colonies with no taxation either for a number of years. England had a monopoly over Scotland because of trading laws for long enough, if they could do it, so could Scotland[129]. English opposition to Scotland trading independently only encouraged the Scot's to invest more money, some to their last penny. Scotland even turned to other countries for investment and even this was blocked by William[130]. The Scot's then viewed this as an opportunity to go it alone with their

---

[127] J MacLehose *Scottish History & Life* (J Patton, 1902, p 134)
[128] W Moffat *A History of Scotland*, book 4 (1985, p 17)
[129] H Brown *A Short History of Scotland* (1951, p 283)
[130] W Moffat *ibid* (1985, p 17)

Darien Scheme. Overall things looked prosperous for Scotland, the Scot's would be free from restrictive trading laws enforced by England and Scotland alone would reap the benefits. It is estimated that nearly half of Scotland's wealth was invested; such was their confidence in this opportunity[131]. The first expedition left from the pier of Leith and reached its destination[132] in November 1698; it consisted of five ships and fifteen hundred men with provisions for six months. The majority of trading goods brought where totally unsuitable for trading with the Indians. Blue bonnets were sent from Kilmarnock, plaids from Dunkeld, stockings from Aberdeen while Edinburgh supplied periwigs, tobacco pipes and linen[133]. However, trouble was evident from the very start. Disease broke out amongst the colonists and provisions ran out. On top of this the Spaniards claimed Darien as their property. The Scots were attacked by the Spaniards and William III refused to allow the English neighbouring colonies to help them.

The second expedition arrived in 1700 oblivious to what had happened, realizing the impending failure they rescued who they could and headed back home. Out of three thousand Scot's who set out, only three hundred or so survived[134] out of the two expeditions. This was the end of the Darien scheme; the Scot's through being overzealous and their lack of experience had failed. It was not entirely their fault, William had endorsed the scheme and then turned his back on the whole venture. A riot broke out in Edinburgh smashing windows of those loyal to the Government, the Tolbooth was forced open and the prisoners released. The Lord High Commissioner had his coach windows smashed; he was then pulled out the coach near the Tron Kirk and dragged up the High Street[135]. Luckily for him he was saved by friends who were armed. The bells of St Giles Cathedral were ringing to a tune accompanied by the mob singing "Wilful Willie, will thou be wilful still"[136]. William hated the freedom of speech in

[131] J Prebble *The Lion in the North* (1981, p 285)
[132] W M Mackenzie *Outline of Scottish History* (1916, p 359) mentioned that they settled in "The Bay of Acia, now Caledonia Bay, North of the Gulf of Darien"
[133] H Brown *A Short History of Scotland* (1951, p 506-507)
[134] C Thomson *Scotland's Work and Worth*. Volume 1(1909, p 258)
[135] D Butler *The Tron Kirk of Edinburgh* or *Christ's Kirk at the Tron* (1906, p 63-64)
[136] H Brown *ibid* (1951, p 284)

Scotland mainly because of their independent Parliament and he expressed the wish "that Scotland were a thousand miles from England, and that he were never the king of it"[137].

Turmoil between two nations

Both Scotland and England were unsettled by the failure of the Darien scheme. Scotland had invested heavily and it had brought ruin to thousands from Peers to shopkeepers alike[138]. On the death of William III in 1702 Queen Anne succeeded to the throne. She was the daughter of James VII of Scotland and II of England (1685-1688), the exiled king. Anne was born to a catholic king but she was brought up in the protestant faith. Anne was the last of the Stewart monarchs to reign over Scotland and England and despite 17 pregnancies when she died, there was no issue left to inherit the crown. For almost one hundred years one monarch had reigned over the two kingdoms. In 1701 the English Parliament passed the Act of Settlement. The Act was simple. On Anne's death the crown should go to Sophia, the Electress of Hanover or her issue. Scotland was mortified that they were not even consulted on this delicate matter. Discontentment had been present in Scotland because the monarchs had always lived and ruled from London since 1603. On top of this the English had always asphyxiated Scotland in their trading. The Parliament of Scotland retaliated by passing the Act of Security in 1704, Scotland was still independent and they wanted their neighbours to take notice[139]. The declaration was that if Anne should die without heirs a successor must be chosen within twenty days after her death. The successor must be from the house of Stewart and also a protestant. The only way the English could choose the successor was to allow Scotland to have free trade, religion and their independent Parliament retained. Scotland could have had a separate monarch if they chose the right sovereign. This made England furious and up to this point the English had always treated Scotland with condescending acquiescence. This all changed. The two countries where nearly at war, despite this England then

---

[137] C Thomson *Scotland's Work and Worth*. Volume 1 (1909, p 258)
[138] J MacLehose *Scottish History & Life* (Patton, 1902, p 136)
[139] J MacLehose *ibid* (Patton, 1902, p 137)

passed their Alien Act[140]. This Act declared that if Scotland did not agree to pick a sovereign to rule over both countries by Christmas day 1705, upon Anne's death all Scot's would be treated as foreigners. Matters were serious indeed for both countries. England seized a Scottish ship and Scotland did likewise, seizing an English ship called *The Worcester* in the Firth of Forth[141]. Both Scotland and England were at boiling point. Nevertheless, thirty one commissioners were appointed from each country to come together to assuage the situation.

The Union of Parliaments (1707)

Previous attempts had been made to unite Scotland and England into one nation. In 1603 King James VI and I who fashioned himself as a monarch of Great Britain made an attempt but it failed when negotiations were abandoned. Even after 1689 the Scottish Parliament records are full of discussions on the subject. In 1706 The English Parliament asked the Queen to appoint Commissioners; the Scottish Parliament did likewise to discuss a Union. It is more than likely that Hamilton, Queensbury and Argyll may have had influence on who was chosen[142] certainly all had a pre-disposition to self serving bias. In August 1706 the Duke of Queensbury asked Lord Godolphin for a sum of money. He received £20,000 to be paid out to some of the Scottish nobles amongst others who received nothing. Queensbury himself received £12,325 for arrears on his salary and expenses for being the Queen's Lord High Commissioner[143]; this was an unbelievable amount of money in the early eighteenth century. Eventually there were thirty two Commissioners from Scotland and thirty two from England appointed. Both parties met in London to discuss a treaty. Meetings took place

[140] W M Mackenzie *Outline of Scottish History* (1916, p 382) states that "the Act declared that all Scotsmen not residing in England, Ireland, or the colonies, or serving in the army or navy, should be treated as aliens; forbade the brining of English horses, arms, or ammunition into Scotland".
[141] C Thomson *Scotland's Work and Worth.* Volume 1(1909, p 265)
[142] T I Rae *The Union of 1707 It's impact on Scotland* (Riley, 1974, p 4)
[143] http://www.parliament.uk/actofunion/09_bribery.html In fact, Queensbury's recorded arrears amounted to a staggering £26,756, though it is not known how such a sum was incurred.

over a period of three days and eventually both countries agreed to a treaty. The Scottish Parliament were then to debate wither the treaty should be passed or not. Every town in Scotland was filled with excitement mostly by crowds who displayed acts of contempt for the Union. Personal problems were forgotten to an extent with a focus of antipathy to the Union. In Edinburgh the Duke of Queensbury and the Lord High Commissioner were stoned by a mob[144]. Of course there was polarization within the Scottish Parliament but eventually the treaty was passed on the 16th January. Thus, "The Scot [tish] Privy Council by proclamation dissolved the Scots Parliament on 28th April 1707"[145]. The actual treaty was signed in a cellar or "laigh shop" at 177 High Street[146].

It was on the 1st May 1707 that the Act of Union was fully established. There was no rejoicing in Scotland. Indeed, "the Elders of the Kirk decided that May 1 should be a day of fasting, to atone for the country's humiliation"[147]. There was an attempt to rename both countries North Britain and South Britain however, this failed after a very short time. England and Scotland became one kingdom called Great Britain, all under the Union jack flag[148]. Initial attempts failed to run Scotland from Westminster[149]. Before long positions were appointed to alleviate the problems, Seafield was made Chancellor and the Earl of Mar Secretary of State for Scotland.

So what did the Union do for the Scots?

A parcel of rogues

The sum of £398.85 was to be paid to Scotland to help her trade and make up for the failed Darien scheme. In truth, the majority of

---

[144] H Brown *A Short History of Scotland* (1951, p 289)

[145] R M White & I D Willock *The Scottish Legal System 3RD edition* (1999, p 28)

[146] D Butler *The Tron Kirk of Edinburgh* or *Christ's Kirk at the Tron* (1906, p 64)

[147] C S Stevenson *Inglorious Rebellion The Jacobite Risings of 1708, 1717 and 1719* (1973, p 57)

[148] The Saltire is said to be one of the oldest national flags of any country, dating back at least to the 12th century.

[149] T I Rae *The Union of 1707 It's impact on Scotland* (Riley, 1974, p 20)

folk who received any of this money were the big investors of the Darien scheme. It obviously goes without saying that a lot of the big investors wanted their money back whatever the cost. No one could summarize the whole episode better that Scotland's famous bard Robert Burns[150].

> *What force or Guile could not subdue,*
> *Thro' many warlike ages,*
> *Is wrought now by a coward few,*
> *For hireling traitors wages.*
> *The English steel we could disdain,*
> *Secure in valour's station;*
> *But English gold has been our bane,*
> *Such a parcel of rogues in a nation.*

The majority of Scot's viewed this as nothing more than a bribe, and with good reason. The money was also to be paid immediately but it was not until the 5th August that the wagons filled with cash and a contingent of Dragoons reached Edinburgh. To add insult to injury only one quarter of the money was in cash the rest in Exchequer bills[151].

Intrusion on Scotland's religion and law

The Church of Scotland was to remain Presbyterian. However, Scotland's churches were interfered with. Scotland still retained their courts according to Article 12 of the Treaty, or so the Scots thought. In 1709 an Episcopalian clergyman by the name of Green-Shields was put in prison by the Court of Session for using the English book of prayer in Scotland[152]. Episcopalians believed that the King had a divine right and the Church should rule through the King or Queen via the Bishops whereas Presbyterians believed that Christ was the head of

---

[150] R Burns *The complete illustrated poems, songs & ballads of Robert Burns* (1990, p 409)
[151] C S Stevenson *Inglorious Rebellion The Jacobite Risings of 1708, 1717 and 1719* (1973, p 59)
[152] R Mackie *A Short History of Scotland* (1947, p 339)

the Kirk (church). Green-Shields appealed to the House of Lords in England and had his appeal sustained, He was then released from prison. This obviously infuriated the Scottish Court because they had been overruled by an English court; despite all this no breach had been done to the Treaty. Appeals in the past had been put to the Scottish Parliament. There was only one Parliament now, the British Parliament which was based in London[153].

Scottish laws where ignored to a certain degree, "the English judges and council, however learned in the common law, lacked detailed knowledge of Scots Law"[154]. English law was based on the doctrine of Parliamentary Sovereignty;[155] whereas Scotland was not. Even as late as 1806 Lord Chancellor Erskine, who was a Scotsman by birth, confessed to the House of Lords "I know something of the law but of Scotch law I am as ignorant as a native of Mexico; and yet I am quite as learned in it as any of your lordships", [156].

New taxes

The Union brought with it an influx of English excise men and customs officers. The same weights and measures were to be used and "part of the agreement [which] apparently was shelved after 1709 was that Scotland was to retain its mint in Edinburgh for the local coinage of money. New taxes were introduced in Scotland. Only Englishmen were sent into the Highlands to collect the taxes, again resulting in more acrimony.

The new taxes which were introduced affected the Scottish economy with disastrous results. In 1712 the fishing industry was almost ruined due to the Salt tax. In 1713 the Malt tax introduced through the Treaty of Utrecht[157] caused fierce riots in Glasgow. One Member of Parliament Campbell of Shawfield had his mansion looted

---

[153]T I Rae *The Union of 1707 It's impact on Scotland* (Murray, 1974, p 46) mentions "no doubt to teach both Scottish Presbyterians and English non-conformists a lesson"
[154] T I Rae *ibid* (Murray, 1974, p 47)
[155] Parliamentary Sovereignty is where a legislative body or Government has absolute power. There is no appeal and prior legislative acts could also be repealed by implication.
[156] A D Gibb *Law from over the Border* (1950, p 49)
[157] C D Murray *Duncan Forbes of Culloden* (1936, p 40)

mainly because he was one of the Whigs who had voted for the tax[158]. Ironical that it was the Whigs who done the looting. Malt was one of the main ingredients for the production of ale, which was the main drink of the common folk. Although the Malt Act was passed it proved too difficult to enforce in Scotland[159]. This was due to the fact that there was too much opposition therefore it become more prudent not to enforce this tax. In 1713 the Earl of Marchmont infuriated at this tax, proposed that the Treaty of Union should be repealed at the House of Lords, his motion was lost by only four votes[160]. Scotland's industries were asphyxiated. This sorry state of affairs had all come about simply because the majority of voters in the new Parliament were English[161].

Anti Union and Jacobite literature

In 1686 James VII set up and made James Watson (1664-1722) the Kings publisher. This fervent Jacobite had a respectable publishing firm in Craig's Close Edinburgh. He published various pamphlets reflecting political interests and his personal economic concerns for Scotland. Watson was summoned before the Privy Council in 1700 for his publication '*The people of Scotland's Groans and Lamentable Complaint Pour'd out before the High Court of Parliament*'[162]. He managed to argue his case against the Williamite Government that the publication was admittedly of 'ill design' but it was also done through necessity to feed his large family. In 1705 Watson was in trouble again for the ballad "*A pill for the Pork Eaters or a Scots lancet for an English swelling*" part of which contained the following words[163].

> "*Then England for its treachery should mourn,*
> *Be forced to fawn, and truckle in its turn:*
> *Scots Pedlars you no longer durst upbraid*

---

[158] H G Graham *The Social Life of Scotland in the Eighteenth Century* (1928, p 526)
[159] H Brown *A Short History of Scotland* (1951, p 292)
[160] R Mackie *A Short History of Scotland* (1947, p 340)
[161] T I Rae *The Union of 1707 It's impact on Scotland* (Riley 1974, p 18)
[162] R T Skinner *The Royal Mile* (1947, p 97)
[163] T I Rae *ibid* (Ross & Scobie, 1974, p 97) Ross and Scobie have given this as a quotation from J Prebble *The Darien Disaster* (1970 p 18)

And DARIEN should with interest be repaid"

Watson was perhaps one of the first to express his patriotic opinions in such a treacherous political environment.

Around the time of the Union Scottish "cultural fragmentation" was also expressed in the republication of works by Barbour's *Bruce* and Blind Harry's *Wallace*[164]. In 1713 news papers and papers full of Jacobite sympathy were freely distributed and there was disorder amongst Jacobites in Leith. Some of these writings may have been done by Watson or Allan Ramsay who started writing patriotic poetry in 1712. Ramsay was also the first person to found the first travelling library in Britain later in his life. Arguably, England had a wider distribution of Jacobite sentiments on paper. The following poem is taken from Monod's work *Jacobitism and the English people, 1688-1788*[165].

Appear Oh James! Approach thy native shore
And to their an[c]ient State thy Realms restore
When thou arrives this nauseous tribe will fly
Right shall revive and usurpation dye

Jacobite poem from 1720

The mistrust by Scot's from the Darien Scheme, the Union and politics carried on for many years. Even in the late 1720s Burt met a clan chief who was walking in the grounds of his house alone armed with a dirk, a pistol at his side and a gun in his hand. Burt does not mention the clan chiefs' name but he does indicate his manner was "as if he feared to be assassinated"[166]; These factors may have simmered down to a point but there was still the roads being built after the failed rising of 1715. Such was the trepidation for many folk in Scotland.

---

[164] T I Rae *The Union of 1707 It's impact on Scotland* (Ross & Scobie, (1974, p 94-95)
[165] P K Monod *Jacobitism and the English people, 1688-1788* (1993, p 45)
[166] Edward Burt *Letters from a Gentleman in the North of Scotland to His Friend in London* Volume 1 (1754, p 56)

Arguably, from an English perspective, "the chief objective behind the Union was the future succession of the House of Hanover"[167]. Almost certainly the state of affairs in Scotland was not just because of the Darien scheme and the unpopular Union. Scottish nobility was always influenced by their political, social and economic pressures. Many of those possessing wealth and entrepreneurial instincts moved to London or the colonies for what they believed was a better life.

---

[167] http://www.parliament.uk/actofunion/uk_01_consolidating.html

Chapter V

Ruffians, rogues and rascals

Like all societies there were the ruffians, rogues and rascals who did not care for gentlemanly ways. When Burt stated "Sometimes, when a company of them have previously resolved and agreed to be peaceably and friendly over their *usky*, they have drawn their dirks and stuck them all into the table before them"[168]. On this particular occasion there was to be no backstabbing or private stabbings at the table. Back stabbing in those days meant just that, rather than the verbal association we have nowadays. The Highland custom of sticking your dirk into the table was likely to be carried out amongst the ruffians of the day. At big assemblies for example, weddings or funerals there was much drunkenness and "much mischief done among them"[169]. One could interpret Burt's use of the word 'mischief' to mean 'rough play' or a situation getting slightly out of hand.

The most common drink amongst the peasantry was two-penny ale or beer preferably laced with *usky* or brandy. Water was on the whole unsafe to drink no matter where it came from. Ale was not consistent in quality and therefore often unpleasant to the palate. Brandy and wine were often consumed, smuggled or stolen from the Lowlands, especially in Fife. On one particular raid by soldiers and excise officials in St Andrews eleven hundred gallons of brandy were confiscated. Forbes of Culloden had a part in this but then again Forbes did not have to worry about the price of liquor on his table[170].

Whisky was a common drink in the Highlands, distilled in the Glens and drunk by all, in 1700 it was 10d a quart. As Graham mentioned "In all transactions the free trader was a hero; to jink the

---

[168] Edward Burt *Letters from a Gentleman in the North of Scotland to His Friend in London* Volume 2 (1754, p 223)

[169] Edward Burt *ibid* (1754, p 224)

[170] C D Murray *Duncan Forbes of Culloden* (1936, p 95) mentions that, "the country of Fife seems to have been a notorious place for smuggling in huge consignments of wine and brandy under the very noses of the revenue officials".

gauger was an honorable exploit"[171]. Murray has an enthralling story taken from Montrose's papers[172] "a gauger (exciseman) came upon ten or twelve Clan Donald drovers refreshing themselves behind a dyke. Relying unwisely on the army's distant presence, the gauger thought to put these Hielan tykes in their place. He declared the gathering a public session with tax due on the whisky, which he tried to confiscate. Unluckily for him he was not seen as a fellow Scot but an officer of the usurping 'German lairdie'. The MacDonalds forced him on to his knees, made him drink a quaich of their whiskey to the health of King James VIII" and then they cut of one of his ears. Nonetheless, it was not until around 1750 that whisky was seen with regularity in the Lowlands. Despite widespread smuggling being carried out certain crimes were most uncommon burglary for example was practically unheard of in both the Lowlands and the Highlands[173].

The witch hunters

There also appeared to be outbreaks relating to the prosecution of witches in Fife[174] these could have been linked to the smuggling operations and the smugglers nocturnal behaviour. Witchcraft was used to explain a bad harvest or perhaps a sudden illness, indeed anything that could not be logically explained. For example in 1704 in Pittenweem a boy became subject to uncontrollable fits. One unfortunate woman was accused of inflicting these fits on the boy by sorcery[175]. She was flung into the hole which was a confined, damp and cold dungeon. This was a dreadful place for the retention of so called criminals. She eventually confessed to the crimes against her after five days without sleep and being subject to the Witchprickers torture. Five months then passed for her case to be brought before the Privy Council. Luckily for her some members of the Council arranged an escape for the poor woman. This is one of the rare examples were the punishment was not approved immediately which was normally

---

[171] H G Graham *The Social Life of Scotland in the Eighteenth Century* (1928, p 528)
[172] W H Murray *Rob Roy MacGregor His life and Times* (1982, p 166)
[173] H Brown *A Short History of Scotland* (1951, p 500-502)
[174] W M Mackenzie *Outline of Scottish History* (1916, p 417)
[175] H G Graham *ibid* (1928, p 486)

66

the case. As can be seen those suspected of witchcraft were put under extreme torture to extract a confession. In Lanarkshire 12 witches were burnt at the stake. At Prestonpans between 1563 and in 1727, 81 witches were prosecuted. Incidentally the last witch to be burnt at the stake in Scotland was in 1727. The link in this chapter is with the witchprickers who plied their evil profession on any poor, vulnerable victim. They were employed by the Town Council and the Court of Session.

Highway robbery in Scotland

Marshall Wade was commissioned with the construction of military roads in the north of Scotland in between 1724 and 1736. Any travelling done before the roads were built was accomplished by means of dirt tracks or trails if there were any. Two lines were struck up near Fort William which was apparently well known in the area[176].

"Had you seen these roads before they were made,
You would hold up your hands and bless General Wade"

Pack-roads were few and far between towns and coaches were predominantly a luxury of the rich. This also meant that there was virtually no such thing as a highwayman or robber in the Highlands. Graham mentions with humour that "they would have grown weary of waiting for passengers to waylay, and died of poverty from finding so little to plunder from their persons"[177]. Burt and a servant travelled throughout the Highlands of Scotland several times carrying four or five hundred guineas with no threat whatsoever in the 1720s[178]. Johnson also commented that the roads are safe both day and night, "where there are so few travellers, why should there be robbers"[179]. Johnson's observation was of course made after the pacification of the

[176] H Brown *A Short History of Scotland* (1951, p 297)
[177] H G Graham *The Social Life of Scotland in the Eighteenth Century* (1928, p 48)
[178] Edward Burt *Letters from a Gentleman in the North of Scotland to His Friend in London* Volume 2 (1754, p 238) also wrote that "I wish we could say as much of our own Country, civilized as it is said to be"
[179] Samuel Johnson *A journey to the Western Islands of Scotland* (1773, p 30)

Highlands in 1773. Even in the Lowlands it was not until 1749 that the first stagecoach journeyed between Edinburgh and Glasgow.

The beginning of pacification in the Highlands

Garrisons with connecting roads were built by Wade at Fort George, Fort Augustus, Fort William, Crieff and Inverness to pacify the wild Highlanders. The total length of the roads came to approximately two hundred and sixty miles. The roads were built to help enforce the Act passed in 1725 commanding that all arms were to be taken from Highland clans who still had Jacobite sympathies. However, this Act was given the same disregard as the previous disarming Act of 1716. This Disarming Act was a direct result of the 1715 rising by the Earl of Mar. Some weapons after implementation of both these Acts were handed in but all in all most of these arms were broken and of no use to the Highlanders[180]. Murray also mentions that regular trade was set up around 1716 between Scotland and Holland which supplied many of these obsolete weapons to be handed over to the Government. John Forbes of Culloden gave his signature for two lists of arms, one from the Burgh of Inverness and the other for the County[181]; interestingly no dirks were mentioned in the inventory. Good serviceable weapons were, without doubt, greased down to prevent rust and hidden in their roof thatches, or other secret places for later use.

The history books are full of treacherous and notorious characters so one can only give a few examples that captivated me. Clan feuds were common throughout the Highland and Lowland clans of Scotland. For many clans intermarriages were a method of ensuring safety from a neighbouring more powerful clan. Or in some cases they

---

[180] C D Murray *Duncan Forbes of Culloden* (1936, p 25)
B Lenman *The Jacobite Risings in Britain 1689-1756* (1980, p 210)
[181] C D Murray *ibid* (1936, p 27) One list contained "162 guns valued at £96, 14s. 2d. and a miscellaneous assortment of guns without locks, gun barrels, side pistols, swords a target and a danesaxe which brought his bag to the respectable total of £106, 7s. 6d".The other list contained "60 guns, reinforced by 4 guns without locks, 3 pairs of pistols, 2 barrels and a lock, a danesaxe, a two handed sword, 36 ordinary swords and 7 targets". The total value of this cache was £34, 12s. 2d.

were used to obtain an inheritance or hold onto one as in the case of MacLean of Duart and Lord Lovat.

Lachlan MacLean of Duart

One clan leader Lachlan MacLean of Duart married a sister of the Earl of Argyle[182]. The marriage was an unhappy one and after some time there was no forth coming pregnancy either. MacLean suspected his wife to be barren. He decided to get rid of her so he had his wife abducted and tied to a rock between the islands of Lismore and Mull by some of his clansmen. The rock used to be known as the rock of Lersker but after MacLean's deed it became known as Lady's Rock[183]. The intention was plain, murder; inevitably she would drown when the tide came in. A few days later MacLean filled with grief and tears, approached his brother in law the Earl of Argyle to inform his in-laws of the tragic accidental drowning of his wife. What MacLean did not know is that a fishing boat had passed by the rock and rescued his wife from her terrible fate. His wife had immediately set of for refuge with her kin and informed them of MacLean's nefarious intention to get rid of her. Revenge was exacted later with MacLean being dirked to death while he was in bed in Edinburgh at the hands of her brother Sir John Campbell of Calder[184].

Simon Fraser (Lord Lovat)

Another notorious Highlander was Simon Fraser (1676-1747) or Lord Lovat. His aim in life was to become "the Lord Lovat that ever was" and no one could deny that to an extent he achieved this through his infamy[185]. He was born in Inverness but the exact date of his birth has not been established however, consensus is around the year

---

[182] A Fulton *Scotland and her Tartans* (1991, p 151) this was in the early 16th century however; he was such a good example of a rogue, ruffian or rascal that I had to include him in this chapter.
[183] T R Barnett *Scottish Pilgrimage in the Land of Lost Content* (1942, p 45-46)
[184] R R McIan *Costumes of the Clans of Scotland* (1845, p 225)
[185] W C Mackenzie *Lovat of the Forty-five* (1934, p 9)

1676^{186}. Simon was educated at the University of Aberdeen where he distinguished himself with a Master of Arts degree. His elder brother Alexander had been present at the raising of the standard for Bonnie Dundee in 1689. Alexander later killed an antagonist during a funeral at Beauly near Inverness. He then fled to Wales to avert the punishment for his crime where he died 1692. After Simon's education he became a Jacobite spy while serving for Prince William. Not long into his service he was put under a court marital for treason but he managed to get himself acquitted. There was a dispute as to the title of the estates after the death of the 8th Lord Lovat who died in 1696^{187}. The estates were in danger of being lost to the immediate family and Simon was the rightful heir to the Fraser of Lovat estates[188]. Simon had to marry the Dowager Lady to hold on to the property. The dispute was between The Master of Saltoun and Simon himself. Saltoun was chosen to marry the Dowager Lady. Simon would have none of this so with some clansmen he kidnapped Saltoun and held him in a tower. Simon then erected a gallows in front of his captors threatening to hang Saltoun[189]. This scheme worked for Simon as Saltoun eventually broke down and gave written confirmation that he was relinquishing his marriage to the Dowager Lady. Simon's next move was a disgraceful act that haunted him for the rest of his life. He kidnapped the Dowager Lady and forced her into marriage. The consummation took place while a piper was playing to drown the screams of Simon's bride.

Meanwhile Saltoun had appealed to the Marquis of Atholl who raised a force against Simon and his father, Thomas Fraser of Beaufort. It is not sure to what extent his father played a part. However, both did not appear before the Privy Council to the charges of High Treason brought against them. Since neither appeared in court they were deemed to be guilty and the sentence of death was passed. Lady Dowager was then reluctantly rescued from her abduction and refrained from ever seeing her husband again. This tells a story itself, what did Simon do to win her over, since she was reluctant to leave?

[186] W C Mackenzie *Outline of Scottish History* (1934, p 10)
[187] A K Campsie *The MacCrimmon Legend* (1980, p 30)
[188] B Lenman *The Jacobite Cause* (1986, p 39)
[189] W C Mackenzie *ibid* (1934, p 10)

We will never know. Simon, his father and clansmen disappeared to
Dunvegan in Skye, the ancestral home of the Macleod's.
The Macleod's and the Lovat Frasers were allies through Thomas
being a brother in law to the clan chief of the Macleod's. Simon later
inherited his title in 1699 when his father died. Around this time
Simon went over to France where he gained sufficient credit as a
Jacobite at the exiled Court of St. Germains[190]. The charge of rape was
later dropped to a lesser charge against Simon because the principle
witness (his wife) would not appear in court. Simon then came back
over to Scotland as a Hanoverian. Upon his return Lovat's clan
deserted him thinking he was totally loyal for the Hanoverian cause.
Lovat was so convincing regarding the Hanoverian cause that George I
agreed to be his eldest son's Godfather[191]. While he played no active
Jacobite part in the rising of 1715 he dubiously acted as a spy sifting
out the Highland chiefs loyal to the Stuart restoration[192], Lovat's
clansmen later changed their allegiance.

In 1734 Lovat managed to obtain a legal settlement costing £12,000
Lovat then had clear title to the entire estate[193]. It is possible that the
two Scottish Judges, Lord Grange and Lord Duns were predisposed in
their decision for Lovat. Lady Grange the wife to Lord Grange was
abducted two or three years earlier. At the time no one knew who the
kidnappers were. More than likely they were Lovat's clansmen. She
was taken to St Kilda amongst other locations but was eventually held
captive at Dunvegan in Skye, Macleod's abode. Lady Grange was a
drunken, bad tempered woman was on the verge of insanity. She was
also rumored to have intelligence about the Jacobite clan leaders. Not
long after the abduction, Lord Grange mourned for his wife's demise.
The Highlanders were well used to keeping secrets, years later Lady
Grange died due to own abusive life style. It was later rumored that
Lovat had designed the whole escapade with Sir Alexander
MacDonald; which he probably did. Lovat being a rogue obviously
denied having anything to do with it.

---

[190] W M Mackenzie *Outline of Scottish History* (1916, p 379)
[191] http://www.annongul.i12.com/page_11.htm
[192] C W Thomson *Scotland's Work and Worth* Volume 1 (1909, p 314-315)
[193] A K Campsie *The MacCrimmon Legend.* (1980, p 31)

Finally, when he was at a good old age, attestations were provided for his part in the 1745-46 Jacobite rising[194]. He was arrested by Captain Ferguson and taken to London where he was put on trial at Westminster Hall. John Murray of Broughton (the Prince's own secretary) and Lovat's secretary provided the main body of evidence against Lovat. Murray had turned into an informer to save his own head. On the 9th of April 1747 he was beheaded on the Tower Hill. As a matter on interest Lovat refused to petition the King for mercy-he preferred to go out under the executioners axe than to have a lingering death caused by illness brought on by old age.

Robert Roy MacGregor (Raibert Ruadh)

Robert Roy MacGregor or in Gaelic Raibert Ruadh (1671-1734) without a doubt was a rogue of infamous disposition. He was the third son of Donald Glas of Glengyle and Margaret Campbell, his father was a senior member of the clan MacGregor. Rob named after his red (*Ruadh*) hair was a man of even temperament who unlike many of his day actually cared for others around him. Rob soon became famous for his cattle's dealing's up and down the country. Owners of property and cattle would pay their "Black rent" to the likes of Rob who was paid to protect their cattle from theft. He was particularly noted for raiding cattle in the Athol region which was property of Lord Murray. In January 1693 he married Mary Helen Campbell of Comar. When she became pregnant he sought to deal in a more honest business. Believing he would receive a customary pardon from Lord Murray Rob signed a bond along with Glengarry and Alasdair Og. Bonds of this nature were often given amongst chiefs and chieftains of a clan. The bond was security for peaceful behaviour and if this good behaviour was broken a sum of one thousand pounds would be paid to his Lordship. As a matter of interest Simon Fraser the next Lord Lovat was one of the witness's to the bonds signatures. The bond was not accepted by Lord Murray and sometime later Rob and his accomplices

---

[194] After the battle of Prestonpans the Prince's secretary John Murray of Broughton and Cluny MacPherson signed and brought Lovat a letter in the Prince's own Handwriting offering the command of the Jacobite Army which Lovat did not accept.

were imprisoned in the Tolbooth in Glasgow. On the 19th December 1695 the Privy Council sentenced him to serve in Flanders[195] along with some of his imprisoned friends. However, Rob and his friends escaped, possibly through bribery in one form or another.

The first decade of the 18th century brought poverty to many and this period has often been referred to as the 'hungry years'[196]. In 1712 Rob borrowed one thousand pounds from James Grahame the 1st Duke of Montrose[197] (second creation in 1707) to finance his cattle droving and to help his fellow kin. The money once received, was either stolen or lost, one thing is for sure it was never recovered or heard of again. Montrose giving no deliberation sought a warrant that was given on 3rd October for Rob's arrest as a notorious bankrupt and outlaw[198].

Rob's property at Graigrostan was seized by Graham of Killearn who was also Montrose's Deputy Sheriff and a contingent of Government troops. His wife Mary was more than likely beaten. Whether she was raped and branded on the check with a hot iron is a contentious issue. Rob and his family therefore found refuge from the Earl of Breadlbane (Montrose's nemesis) in Glen Dochart. Rob went back to his old ways concentrating his efforts on cattle thieving and stealing collected rent money from Montrose's estates. Around this time Rob Roy's compassion for others less fortunate is evident by his generosity to the poor. This continued for the next eight years with Rob also being captured but escaping on two or three occasions. Rob managed to obtain a cottage back in Balquhidder in 1720.

Rob Roy fought at Killicrankie (1689) and he played a small but elusive part at Sheriffmuir (1715) probably due to his alliance with the Duke of Argyle. Stevenson mentions that Rob Roy was late in getting to the battle. Therefore he waited "to see the probable winner before committing himself, [he then] marched his clan away for the simple reason that he could perceive no winner"[199], Rob also fought at

---

[195] W H Murray *Rob Roy MacGregor His life and Times* (1982, p 151-156)

[196] H G Graham *The Social Life of Scotland in the Eighteenth Century* (1928, p 228-231)

[197] James received his peerage for his important contribution to the Act of Union while he was Lord President of the Scottish Privy Council

[198] W H Murray *ibid* (1982, p 151)

[199] C S Stevenson *Inglorious Rebellion The Jacobite Risings of 1708, 1717 and 1719* (1973, p 156)

Glenshiel. Daniel Defoe who wrote '*Robinson Crusoe*' was also the Author of '*The Highland Rogue*' in 1723 which made Rob Roy a legend in his own lifetime. It is also possible that the book influenced George I to give Rob his pardon in 1726. On 28th December 1734 the legendary Rob Roy MacGregor passed away peacefully in his cottage at Balquhidder while a piper purportedly played the tune ' *Ha til mi tulidh* ' I shall return no more. From a Hanoverian standpoint every Jacobite was a rebel and of notorious character. However, Rob Roy left the rest of the Clan MacGregor with a certain amount of humanity, honour and dignity.

Authors Sketch of Rob Roy's
Tomb stone
At Balquhidder Church Perthshire

James Macpherson

Another notorious rogue was James Macpherson who was the leader of a gang which was variously referred to as "Egyptians, sorners, cairds, tinkers or gypsies"[200]. Macpherson "was the illegitimate son of a Highland laird, MacPherson of Invereshie, and a beautiful tinker-gypsy girl James's father met at a wedding"[201]. Macpherson operated his band of men around Elgin, Forres and Banff. Macpherson and his associates would attend markets and fairs. They would keep an eye out for any person who appeared to be alone and with a full purse or sporran. Macpherson and his men would then follow their victim or hide and wait for their opportunity to steal their cash or goods they had bought.

Occasionally, the victim would be held captive and held to ransom. One famous person kidnapped by a band of these men was Adam Smith (1723-1790) who is regarded as the first person to write on modern economics[202].

Macpherson was captured in November 1700. Macpherson is reputed to have "incurred the enmity of the rich lairds and farmers of the low country of Banff and Aberdeenshire, and especially of a brash go-getter Duff of Braco who organized a posse to catch him. At Saint Rufus Fair in Keith he was attacked by Braco's men, and was captured after a fierce fight. (According to the traditional account, a woman dropped a blanket over him from a window, and he was disarmed before he could get free of it)"[203]. In the same month (November) Macpherson was condemned to death by hanging. He was by all accounts regarded as a great swordsman and fiddler in his time. During

---

[200] H G Graham *The Social Life of Scotland in the Eighteenth Century* (1928, p 230)
[201] http://www.clandavidsonusa.com/macphersonsrant.htm
[202] Rae John *Life of Adam Smith* (1895, p5) "[W]hile [Adam was] on a visit to his grandfather's house at Strathendry on the banks of the Leven, the child was stolen by a passing band of gipsies, and for a time could not be found. But presently a gentleman arrived who had met a gipsy woman a few miles down the road carrying a child that was crying piteously. Scouts were immediately despatched in the direction indicated, and they came upon the woman in Leslie wood. As soon as she saw them she threw her burden down and escaped".
[203] http://www.clandavidsonusa.com/macphersonsrant.htm The author would like to point out there is other anecdotes regarding Macpherson and his capture.

his incarceration he composed a tune and played it on his fiddle before he was hung. Robert Burns wrote the following song which in a sense gives Macpherson immortality[204].

McPherson's Farewell

Farewell, ye dungeons dark and strong,
The wretch's destinie !
MacPherson's time will not be long
On yonder gallows tree.

Chorus.- Sae rantingly, sae wantonly
Sae dauntingly gaed he
He play'd a spring, and he dan'cd it round,
Below the gallows-tree

O what is death but parting breath?
On many a bloody plain
I've dared his face, and in this place
I scorn him yet again!
Sae rantingly, &c.

Untie these bands from my hands,
And bring to me my sword;
And there's no a man in all Scotland,
But I'll brave him at a word.
Sae rantingly, &c.

I've liv'd a life of sturt and strife;
I die by treacherie:
It burns my heart I must depart,
And not avenged be.
Sae rantingly, &c.

---

[204] R Burns *The complete illustrated poems, songs & ballads of Robert Burns* (1990, p 352)

Now farewell light, thou sunshine bright.
May coward shame disdain his name,
The wretch that dare not die!
Sae rantingly, &c.

Sung to the tune Macpherson's Rant

    After Macpherson had played his tune he then is said to have asked the audience if anyone would accept his instrument. No one stepped forward, he is said to have broken the fiddle over his knee cursing the spectators as he done so.

Chapter VI

Crime & punishment

Many of the punishments inflicted in the 17th and 18th centuries were just clearly not justifiable especially in the Lowlands of Scotland where the population regarded themselves as more civilized. A person convicted of thieving a loaf of bread could be banished from his burgh for a period of one year. Some were publicly whipped after removing their upper garments in Stripping Close in Edinburgh[205]. Others may be put into slavery or the stocks for up to three months and yet some were even sentenced to death. In contrast, Scottish criminal law did have a more compassionate and logical system compared to that of England[206].

Highlanders had nothing but contempt for the 'Lowland laws' as they called them[207]. Miscreants were dealt with harshly by Highlanders and Lowlanders alike and one common punishment was to have a sign in bold letters hanging from one's neck explaining to passers by the crime committed. Criminals would also be locked up in the pillory exposed to public abuse with their ear or lug nailed to the frame. On being released from this punishment the miscreant had no option but to tear their ear away from the frame or if they were fortunate enough a sympathetic person would give them a knife to cut their lug loose. Banishment was another option the courts could impose on those convicted. The ultimate penalty imposed was death by hanging or being beheading. However; it was the state of the jails that inflicted the most harm on those that were unfortunate to be imprisoned. Prisons were dark, unsanitary and therefore full of vermin. Food was very basic to say the least and many a prisoner never came out the same after their fine was paid or sentence was finished-that is if they came out alive! In some cases a death sentence was escaped by being put

---

[205] R T Skinner *The Royal Mile* (1947, p 10)

[206] T I Rae *The Union of 1707 It's impact on Scotland* (Murray 1974, p 44)

[207] Edward Burt *Letters from a Gentleman in the North of Scotland to His Friend in London* Volume 1 (1754, p 236)

into slavery in Scotland, this happened to four people convicted at Perth[208].

Maggie Dickson

A sad case with a happy ending is when Maggie Dickson was hanged for concealing her newborn dead baby which was a criminal offence. She was convicted and her punishment was to be hanged in the Grassmarket in Edinburgh on 2nd September 1724. Once Maggie was pronounced dead by a doctor her body was cut down immediately because a fight ensued between doctors, students and her relatives for Maggie's body. At this date of anatomy and medicine the only body's that could be dissected were those taken from the gallows. Fortunately for Maggie her relatives won because on the way to the churchyard in Musselburgh her relatives stopped for refreshments at a village called Pepper Mill. Someone thought they seen the coffin lid move and on approaching the coffin a banging was heard from Maggie's coffin. She was alive. The town council could not hang her again as she was officially dead and it was God's will she came back from the dead. Maggie lived for another thirty years or so by the name Half Hangit Maggie. She later had a family and ran an alehouse.

The Colonel

Another anecdote from the Lowlands of Scotland relates to fornication outside of marriage and god forbid adultery. This was in no way tolerated in the Highlands and Lowlands. Burt gives a humorous tale of a married Scot's Colonel who was convicted of this terrible crime. The story can only best be described in Burt's own words. The Colonel was to "stand in a Hair cloth, at the Kirk Door, every Sunday Morning for a whole Year. At the beginning of his penance, he concealed his Face as much as he could, but three or four young

---

[208] H G Graham *The Social Life of Scotland in the Eighteenth Century* (1928, p 492) comments that "One of [the four men was] used as a worker in the silver mines in a glen of Ochils, had round his neck a collar with the inscription : "Alexander Stuart found guilty of theft at Perth the 5th Dec. 1701, and gifted by the justiciars as perpetual servant to Sir J. Areskine of Alloa"

Lasses passing by him, one of them stooped down, and cried out to her Companions, Lord! It's Colonel --------. Upon which he suddenly threw aside his Disguise, and said, Miss, you are right, and if you will be the Subject of it, I will wear this Coat another Twelvemonth"[209]. It is worth mentioning the Colonels sentence was comparatively lenient to many others of this nature. In Banffshire the fine imposed for adultery could be between twenty and forty pounds Scot's.

The Porteous Riot

One famous incident was when two smugglers where caught stealing and this led to become known as the Porteous Riot. The two smugglers, one called Robertson[210] from the Donnachaidh clan who where notorious for their smuggling escapades and his accomplice George Wilson stole around £200 by breaking into the Customs House at Pittenweem, in Fife[211]. They both had previous experience with custom officials who had confiscated their smuggled goods over a period of years. This was their form of retaliation for the money they had lost. Not long after the break-in they were both caught and imprisoned in the Tollbooth in Edinburgh[212]. Both were condemned to death. However, they tried to escape by dislodging the bars in their cell. Wilson the stockier of the two tried to escape first but only managed to get stuck. Wilson was angry with himself because Robertson the lighter of the two could have easily escaped if he went first. On the last Sunday of their impending execution April 14th [213] they were allowed to visit Church which was the custom for condemned criminals. All of a sudden a mob fell upon the guards who were accompanying them to the gallows. Robertson the lighter and

---

[209] Edward Burt *Letters from a Gentleman in the North of Scotland to His Friend in London* Volume 1 (1754, p 232-233)
[210] Donnachie as well as being linked as a Sept of Clan Donnachaidh it is also associated as Septs of the Clans Campbell and Grant of Gartenbeg/Dalvey. http://www.donachiesociety.co.uk/history.html
[211] H Brown *A Short History of Scotland* (1951, p 298)
[212] R T Skinner *The Royal Mile* (1947, p 26) the prison was erected on or before 1561; it was later sold for £200 when a more suitable place was decided at Calton Hill.
[213] W M Mackenzie *Outline of Scottish History* (1916, p 414)

more agile of the two escaped. Wilson was held firm but he did manage to hold onto one of the guards with his teeth to help his companion run to his freedom. Wilson was put back in prison with his execution fixed for the next day. He was executed in the Grassmarket and upon his body being taken down the crowd went into an uproar, some throwing stones at his transgressors. Captain Porteous was in charge of the execution. He lost his temper and ordered his men to open fire[214]. He did have the common sense to order his men to fire over the heads of the crown. This backfired so to speak on Porteous as numerous persons were injured and around half a dozen were killed looking out of their windows at the commotion down below[215]. The townsfolk of Edinburgh were sympathetic for Wilson, probably because he was one of the smugglers who regularly supplied them with their contraband goods. The townsfolk immediately demanded that Porteous be brought to justice for the injuries and deaths he irrationally caused[216]. He was subsequently sentenced to death by the High Court[217] but was given a reprieve at the last moment. After all he was only carrying out his duties! The night before his reprieve a crowd gathered outside the prison. The town's folk of Edinburgh were not at all happy about the state of affairs. Despite a few squalls by town guards Porteous was dragged by the crowd down to the Bow at the Grassmarket and hanged till he was dead. Without any further aggravation in the streets the crowd quietly dispersed back to their homes. Robertson with reminiscent conjecture perhaps carried out his skulduggery under a synonym in another part of Scotland or perhaps in Ireland. It was not just the ordinary folk who reaped the benefits of these smuggling operations. Gentlemen of all ranks took part in the running of the precious cargoes. This no doubt explains how the excise men had such difficulty in apprehending any culprits. This is probably the reason why the Porteous riot appeared to be lead by persons of influence; expediently none were identified despite a reward of two hundred pounds for information[218] that led to a conviction.

---

[214] H Brown *A Short History of Scotland* (1951, p 299)
[215] C W Thomson *Scotland's Work and Worth* Volume 1 (1909, p 329)
[216] W M Mackenzie *Outline of Scottish History* (1916, p 415)
[217] C W Thomson *ibid* (1909, p 329)
[218] C W Thomson *ibid* (1909, p 330)

82

Clan feuds were often caused by callous irregular justice that was just Highland Law[219]. For example, a clan would stick by their own kin even if one of them was a criminal. In some circumstances another clansman was picked out to take the place of a harbored criminal.

Things are not always as they appear. This narrative will elucidate how the so called scales of justice could also be manipulated.

Colquhoun and MacGregor clan feud

Members of the Colquhoun clan killed two men from the Clan MacGregor who were seeking customary hospitality but were refused. The MacGregors sought shelter in a barn that belonged to the Colquhoun's and it's more than probable they helped themselves to some food. The weather was not in the Macgregor's favour and they had no choice but to abide on Colquhoun land. The Macgregors retaliated by killing two of the Colquhoun clansmen and lifting a substantial amount of cattle. The Macfarlane's were friends and allies with the MacGregors[220] and it has been suggested that the Macfarlane's were partly responsible for the raid on the Colquhoun's[221]. The Macfarlane's received no reprisal at all. The widows of the Colquhouns and other clan women paraded in Stirling exhibiting shirts dipped in animal blood. This was a totally exaggerated show that became known as the 'Slaughter in the Lennox'[222]. It was also conveniently paraded in front of King James IV who apparently could not stomach the sight of blood.

This was the incident that resulted in the Gregarach being proscribed as outlaws. The Act of the Privy Council on the 3rd Of April 1603 forbade the use of the name MacGregor or Gregor[223]. The proscription also meant that anyone still bearing one of these names could not carry arms. The name MacGregor was not even recognized

---

[219] Samuel Johnson *A journey to the Western Islands of Scotland* (1773, p 72)
[220] W M Mackenzie *Outline of Scottish History* (1916, p 247)
[221] D M Macdonald *Scotland's magazine and Country Life The Armourers of Glen Lyon* Volume 60 No 6 (June 1964, p 21)
[222] H Brown *A Short History of Scotland* (1951, p 226)
[223] W H Murray *Rob Roy MacGregor His life and Times* (1982, p 21)

in the courts, meaning that any agreement in or out with the law with a MacGregor was invalid. On the 20th January 1604 sentences were given out by the Court of Justiciary to the MacGregor's, twenty two were hanged and four were beheaded[224]. Many MacGregor's changed their name[225] through fear of retribution and its likely many did not change their name back when the prohibition was eventually lifted. The famous Rob Roy MacGregor used the name Campbell, his mother's maiden name on many occasions. The name MacGregor was given back without further reprisal in 1775[226] to those persons who wished to use the name! Justice was sometimes a harsh reality and some clans would exploit their enemies with cruel exaggerated relish naturally for self serving bias.

---

[224] W H Murray *Rob Roy MacGregor His life and Times* (1982, p 22)
[225] B Lenman *The Jacobite Cause* (1986, p 50)
[226] A Mackie *Scottish Pageantry* (1967, p 169-170)

Chapter VII

Scottish weapons

This chapter is focused on the well known weapons which were associated with Scotland. Documentation exists that many of the Highlanders and Lowlanders went into battle with nothing more than agricultural tools like scythes fixed to the end of a pole. Indeed the clansman going into battle would arguably be armed to the teeth with any implement that could inflict injury. The manufacture of weapons was carried out in all the important towns in the Lowlands and Highlands. Incorporations of craftsmen and Burgh records were established to provide security for certain trades. Books were kept that gave the names of the craftsmen and their subsequent apprentices. On completion of an apprenticeship the test piece was often recorded as well. The test piece was a sample of the apprentices work. Through these records certain towns and names became well known for the manufacture of specific weapons for example, Doune pistols made by Thomas Caddell and John Murdock[227]. Basket hilts made by John Simpson[228] and Thomas Gemmill in Glasgow soon became known as 'Glasgow hilts'. Other weapons used by clansmen were the halberds, made in vast quantities in Edinburgh, poleaxes and there is also the mention of danesaxe's.

The Lochaber axe

The lochaber axe was a weapon which was used from the 16th century onwards and throughout the 17th and 18th century it was used

---

[227] C E Whitelaw *Scottish Arms Makers A biographical dictionary of makers of firearms, edged weapons and armour working in Scotland from the 15th Century to 1870.* (1977, p 42-43)

[228] S Maxwell; T B Lindsay; C Blair; J Wallace; W Reid; J G Scott; A V B Norman *Scottish Weapons. The Scottish Art Review Magazine* Volume 9 No 1, (Scott 1963, p 22)

by the town guards in Edinburgh[229] and also Highlanders[230]. There
is some contention regarding the style of the earlier weapons and what
one would regard as a lochaber axe now[231]. The lochaber axe is a
normally around six feet in length making it primarily a two handed
weapon. The blade of the lochaber axe can vary in length and breadth
roughly around twelve to eighteen inches long and four to six inches in
breadth. The blade is generally curved and in most cases the curve
deepens at the top of the axe to give a sharp point. At the back of the
axe there are two plates of steel welded and fixed around the wooden
pole. On some axes there was an outward curved spike similar to a
bill-hook welded onto the top fixing mount or blade. This could be
used to great effect for pulling horsemen from their saddle[232] as well as
inflicting injury. Caldwell suggests that the name for the weapon
derived from the length of the shaft[233]. It is more likely that the earlier
axes were predominantly made in the Lochaber region, and therefore,
the name stuck to that particular style of weapon. A battle axe is a
single handed weapon which could be easily used on horseback. This
was one of Robert the Bruce's favourite weapons, on the eve of the
Battle of Bannockburn he slew Sir Henry de Bohun the English
champion by cleaving his head with his battle axe, breaking his axe in
the process.

The Jedburgh staff

The Jedburgh staff is another weapon that probably derived its
name from the geographical location where it was initially made. The
earliest reference the author has found dates to1506 for a Jedwort

[229] Dr. D H Caldwell *Scottish Weapons & Fortifications 1100-1800* (1981, p 300) for
a more in-depth study of Scottish axes and long shafted weapons I would
recommend Caldwell's book.
[230] John Wallace *Scottish Swords and Dirks An illustrated reference guide to Scottish
edged weapons* (1970, p,77)
[231] Dr. D H Caldwell *ibid* (1981, p 253)
[232] W MacKay Junior *Some notes on Highland weapons* (1930, p 7)
[233] D H Caldwell *The Scottish Armoury* (1979, p 19)

hede, with gilt by the Royal cutler Robert Selkirk[234]. There are numerous other accounts in the Lowlands to when this weapon was used in the late 16th century[235]. This style of weapon is similar to the lochaber axe. The main difference is the length of the blade. There is no bill-hook but the blade is by far longer, shorter in width and pointed at the top. Interestingly enough the coat of arms for Jedburgh since the 17th century has been a chevalier on a horse holding a Jedburgh staff; [236]arguably the Jedburgh staff is more associated with the Lowlands.

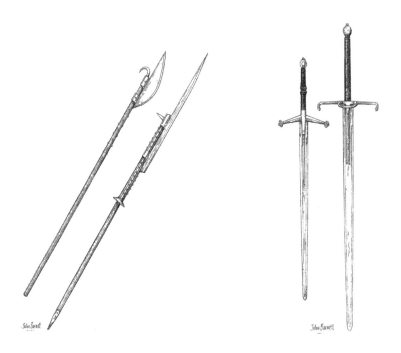

Left to right The Lochaber axe, Jedburgh staff, Claidheamh dà làimh and Lowland sword

[234] C E Whitelaw *Scottish Arms Makers A biographical dictionary of makers of firearms, edged weapons and armour working in Scotland from the 15th Century to 1870.* (1977, p 123)
[235] C E Whitelaw *ibid* (1977, p 20)
[236] http://www.jedburgh-online.org.uk/history.asp

The great two handed sword or *Claidheamh dà làimh*

Two handed swords were being used as far back as the 14th century throughout Europe. Many of these two handed swords would have been used by the likes of mercenaries and bodyguards. Clan chiefs would have them hanging on their great walls as decoration ready to be used at a moment's notice. The Scottish *Claidheamh dà làimh* as it is recognized now first made its appearance around the late 15th century[237]. This is also evident by the large amount of tombstones depicting two handed swords in the Western Highlands and Islands[238]. The weapon was totally distinctive from all other two handed weapons in Europe. The size of a two handed sword could vary from fifty three inches to sixty inches in length, the grip being around twelve inches long. The main features of a *Claidheamh dà làimh* "are the quillons of diamond section angled towards the blade and terminating in quarter foils built up by circles of iron brazed together. The quillon block also has a high collar towards the grip and long tongues extending down the blade"[239]. Wallace indicates that two handed swords with a wheel type pommel are of earlier origin to those with a globular pommel[240]. Any functional two handed weapon has a point of balance normally at the base of the grip and it is surprising to discover how light these great swords actually are. The length of these weapons meant that they were not primarily a stabbing weapon. They were far more devastating when charging at the enemy swinging the sword over the head in a circular or a figure of eight motion. The end of the blade is usually more rounded than other weapons enabling it to slice through flesh and bone with more ease. One example of a *Claidheamh dà làimh* in Drummond's book has the following inscription at the top of the blade[241].

"I WILL VENTER SELFE IN BATEL STRONG

---

[237] D H Caldwell *The Scottish Armoury* (1979, p 26)
[238] M Martin *A Description of the Western Islands of Scotland Circa 1695* (1703, p 141)
[239] John Wallace *Scottish Swords and Dirks An illustrated reference guide to Scottish edged weapons* 1970, p,10)
[240] John Wallace *ibid* (1970, p 11)
[241] James Drummond & Joseph Anderson *Ancient Scottish Weapons* (1881, Plate XV)

88

TO VINDICATE MY MASTERS WROING"

Inscriptions on sword blades were often there to encourage the owner to acts of bravery on the battle field. It is not difficult to imagine a young Highlander having to use such a sword for the first time. A sword of such quality would have been passed through the generations and this would inspire acts of courage and bravery to emulate the feats of his forefathers.

Large two handed swords were made and repaired in Edinburgh by the cutler Robert Selkirk amongst others. A cutler was generally a maker of knifes and daggers of all description. Frequent payments were made between 1502-1512 for "the supply and repair of swords of all sizes"[242]. Selkirk must have been an exceptional craftsman because he also made daggers for the King. Rutherfruid was another cutler from Edinburgh who was exceptional in his craft. However, the Rutherford's were more common in the borders where they where famous for making saddles for horses.

Shell-guarded swords of the late 16th and 17th century which were similar in size to the *Claidheamh dà làimh* were also used by the Highlanders and probably Lowlanders alike. This type of sword has the common cross guard and two guards similar to clam shells spanning partly over the grip. Robert Lyell (Lyall) who was a guardmaker and lorimer in Edinburgh admitted as his test piece a 'clam schellit gairdis and ane pair of ribbit gairdis on 9th January 1584[243].

Lowland swords are primarily larger than the two handed swords used throughout the Highlands. The length of these weapons could vary from sixty inches to nearly seventy six inches[244] (over six feet), very analogous to the two handed swords used in Germany. The shell-guarded sword and Lowland sword more often than not have a distinctive globular pommel.

---

[242] C E Whitelaw *Scottish Arms Makers A biographical dictionary of makers of firearms, edged weapons and armour working in Scotland from the 15th Century to 1870* (1977, p 119)
[243] C E Whitelaw *ibid* (1977, p 170)
[244] John Wallace *Scottish Swords and Dirks An illustrated reference guide to Scottish edged weapons* (1970, p 18) Illustration 9 is a fine example measuring 75 1/2 inches in length unfortunately; many of these weapons are not on display.

Blair mentions in Caldwell's book that 19th century antiquaries were responsible for the word claidheamh mòr being associated with only the two handed sword[245]. At the skirmish near Clifton during the 1745 rising Lord George Murray shouted "claymore" [anglicized version of claidheamh mòr] he then "drew his sword and followed by Cluny and his men, fell upon the enemy, who broke and ran"[246]. Any Highlander using a two handed sword would probably not have carried a targe (target) as the *Claidheamh dà làimh* was primarily a two handed weapon. Carrying a targe with straps holding it on the back would make it too cumbersome to wield the sword. Killicrankie was also arguably the last major battle where Highlanders used the *Claidheamh dà làimh.* Two handed swords were becoming redundant making way for the far lighter highland broadsword or backsword. This does not mean that two hander's were totally phased out after Killicrankie. Some would without doubt be carried for ceremony or as a kind of mascot in the battle.

The Scottish basket hilted sword or claidheamh mòr

The basket hilted sword was a natural evolution from the cross styled swords used during the medieval period. With the gauntlet and body armor outdated the simple earlier basket hilted sword provided protection to the hand and wrist in hand to hand combat. Basket hilt swords are distinguished first by the blade, a double edged blade makes the weapon a broadsword whereas a single edged blade makes the sword a backsword.

It is unlikely that the Scottish basket hilted sword derived from the Shiavona which were the used by the guards in Venice in the early 17th century. Drummond and Anderson may have implied this theory[247] however; it was Laking who proposed that the Scottish basket hilt originated from the Shiavona being first introduced through England[248]. In fact there was a distinctive Scottish sword associated with the Scots around the late 1500s. In 1572 there is mention of a pair

---

[245] Dr. D H Caldwell *Scottish Weapons & Fortifications 1100-1800* (1981, p 238)
[246] The Barron Porcelli *The White Cockade* (1949, p 95)
[247] James Drummond & Joseph Anderson *Ancient Scottish Weapons* (1881, p 18)
[248] Sir G Laking *The Armoury of Windsor Castle* (1904, p 217)

of Heland hiltis presumably manufactured in Inverness to be delivered and mounted on sword blades[249]. Blair states that "it is likely enough that it refers to a basket-guard, for there is evidence for the existence of a form of this that was regarded as specifically Highland at only a slighter later date"[250]. Wallace also mentions the term Highland hilt or guard specifically referred to a Scottish basket hilt[251]. It would, therefore, be a convincing argument that Scottish basket hilted swords were commonly known in the Highlands during the latter half of the 16th century. Confusion was also added with the English referring to Irish hilts which were in fact Scottish. As already mentioned, the term 'Irish' was more associated by the use of the Gaelic tongue, Irish and Scots alike[252]. Blair mentions that there is a similarity in early pommel types specific to the Highland *Claidheamh dà làimh* and early basket hilts where the globular pommels are two hollow pieces of iron brazed together[253]. Blair also mentions that swords unchanged with this type of pommel could be dated to around 1560[254]. It would be a fair argument to state that the basket hilt in various forms originated in not just Germany but, England and Scotland as well as Venice. Early references to Scottish swords (presumably basket hilted) are given as "ribbit sword gairdis" two of which were admitted as an essay piece by William Baxter of Edinburgh in 1608[255]. Late 16th and early 17th century swords are difficult to date and it is not until the middle on the 17th century that dating can be more precise to specific Scottish baskets.

The first pictorial evidence for a Highland basket is probably the portrait of a Highland Chieftain by Michael Wright (1660-1670). This type of basket is often referred to as a ribbon hilt or beak nose [256]

---

[249] C E Whitelaw *Scottish Arms Makers A biographical dictionary of makers of firearms, edged weapons and armour working in Scotland from the 15th Century to 1870* (1977, p 252)

[250] Dr. D H Caldwell *Scottish Weapons & Fortifications 1100-1800* (1981, p 157)

[251] John Wallace *Scottish Swords and Dirks An illustrated reference guide to Scottish edged weapons* (1970, p 22)

[252] J Prebble *The Lion in the North* (1981, p 298)

[253] C E Whitelaw *ibid* (1977, p 236)

[254] Dr. D H Caldwell *ibid* (1981, p 216)

[255] C E Whitelaw *ibid* (1977, p 164)

[256] John Wallace *ibid* (1970, p 23)

probably due to the construction of the basket made with ribbons or strips of steel welded together. This type of basket lacks the two forward guards that later baskets obtained. The earlier swords probably had the basket and blade manufactured by the local smiths of the Highlands and Lowlands. The grip was normally of wood with a sharkskin covering bound with brass or silver wire. Some grips were just wood bound with brass or silver wire, or even deer horn. Around the middle of the 17th century there is a prolific amount of imported blades coming into Scotland from Spain and Germany. One will also notice the concentric circle and heart shaped piercings used as decoration on the saltire bar, rear-guard and main knuckle guard at the front of the weapon around this period. Around the middle of the 17th century liners were introduced inside the blade end of the basket. This was made from a piece of deerskin or buff leather and helped give protection to the knuckles. It is not until the 19th century that the liner completely covers the internal portion of the basket, the liner has deteriorated into a piece of red cloth or velvet.

Swords of the 18th century are far easier to date mainly because certain makers of hilts started to mark their work. There is also a far greater amount of Scottish portraits available that have survived the rigors of time. At the beginning of the 18th century imported blades from Germany were being produced with Jacobite references etched into the blade. Wallace refers to these swords in his work *Scottish swords and dirks*; "prosperity to Schotland and no Union" on one side and "For God, My Country, and King James the 8th" on the other side was common[257]. Portraits' of the exiled King, crossed scepters and St Andrew and his cross were other variations on sword blades during the period of the anti union of the Parliaments[258]. Baskets were often browned or sometimes varnished to help with preservation from the harsh climate in Scotland.

---

[257] John Wallace *Scottish Swords and Dirks An illustrated reference guide to Scottish edged weapons* 1970, p 38, plate 27)
[258] A V B Norman The National Trust for Scotland *Culloden The Swords and the Sorrows* (1996, p 32-35 plates1:18. 1:25. 1:26) provide excellent examples of this type of sword.

Around this time there are also the typical Glasgow hilts being made by John Simpson and Thomas Gemmill[259]. The first John Simpson was one of the first to mark his work with his initials under the back-guard. The second John Simpson was appointed Kings Armourer on the 6th July 1715 under the Scottish Privy Seal he was described as deceased on 22nd August 1717. Several swords known to be made by Gemmill have a lion rampant and crown with the letter K. Armourer or Armorer along with his name on the hilt. Gemmill was appointed Kings Armourer following on after Simpson on 18th January 1718 by letters under the Scottish Privy Seal[260].

Without a doubt the most artistic and beautifully crafted Scottish basket hilts were produced in Stirling by John Allan who was journeyman to John Simpson in Glasgow. John Allan senior and Walter Allan are also famed for their outstanding workmanship in the second quarter of the 18th century. One notable difference in all Allan hilts is that the pommel sits in a ring welded at the top of the hilt. Other contemporaries of the time tended to favour fitting the arms of the guard into a shallow grove on the pommel cap[261]. All three Allan's were exceptional in their work; some of the baskets they produced are finely chased with inlay work consisting of brass or silver[262]. One beautifull example is the sword made for Cameron of Lochiel[263]. This must have been made in conjunction with Colin Mitchell who was a Goldsmith worked in Edinburgh around 1727-1753[264]. Both makers

---

[259] S Maxwell; T B Lindsay; C Blair; J Wallace; W Reid; J G Scott; A V B Norman *Scottish Weapons. The Scottish Art Review Magazine* Volume 9 No 1, (Scott 1963, p 22) Scott mentions that there was three armourers baring the same name in Glasgow in the early 18th century, more than likely from the same family.

[260] C E Whitelaw *Scottish Arms Makers A biographical dictionary of makers of firearms, edged weapons and armour working in Scotland from the 15th Century to 1870* (1977, p 217)

[261] S Maxwell; T B Lindsay; C Blair; J Wallace; W Reid; J G Scott; A V B Norman *ibid* (Scott 1963, p 18)

[262] John Wallace *Scottish Swords and Dirks An illustrated reference guide to Scottish edged weapons* (1970, p 44-48)

[263] A V B Norman The National Trust for Scotland *Culloden The Swords and the Sorrows* ((1996, p 33)

[264] A V B Norman *ibid* (1996, p 33 plate 1;22)

marks are inscribed on the basket as well as the stags head representing the Canongate silversmiths.

Basket hilts were not just manufactured in Scotland; England also made them as well as craftsmen in Germany. Two matching silver swords and targets were commissioned by James the 3rd Duke of Perth. One was made for his brother Henry and the other set presented to Prince Charles. Both swords have silver trophies and the Medusas head cast into the construction. The targets have a cast Medusas head with an aperture for a spike[265].

---

[265] A V B Norman (J Moran) The National Trust for Scotland *Culloden The Swords and the Sorrows* (1996, p 46 and p 56)

Scottish broadsword with highland dirk

Sword blades

Another notable difference on swords of this era is that the blades are almost always imported, mainly from Passau and Solingen. The name Andrea Ferrara also became famous on many Scottish blades of the late 17th and 18th century as well as the running wolf and Kings Head mark of Solingen manufacture. It is more than likely that imported blades were used by those of more disposable income. The redundant two handed swords would be kept only for sentimental value and others would have the blades ground down for the lighter basket hilt. Andrea Ferrara was a name associated with great blades of extreme forging and temper. It has been suggested that he originally came to Scotland from Spain after killing an apprentice who spied on him trying to learn his secret forging process. This is just speculation and as it stands there is no evidence in any form that he came to King James V court to set up his workshop. There was an Andria Ferrara working in Venice in the 16th century and his blades were no doubt of superb temper. After his death the German manufacturers in Solingen and Passau capitalized on his name[266], which does have different spellings on the blades. Campbell gives various different spellings on the name Ferrara[267] (Appendix 5). This also gives the indication that these blades were manufactured in various locations and by different smiths over a period of a hundred years or so. Some Ferrara blades have the globe and cross mark found on many swords of the 16th century, the running wolf of Solingen and the Kings Head mark of Johannes Wundes. Mowbray mentions that "In a French work on arms by Monsieur G.R. Maurice Maindron, the mark of the crowned King's head is given as being the mark of Johannes Wundes of Solingen, and the date is put down as being from A.D. 1560-1610"[268]. There is every possibility that the work of Wundes was also copied. Interestingly enough there are swords that have both Ferrara's name and the mark of Wundes[269]. Some blades were curved and the basket often had one of the saltire replaced with a circular loop. It is reasonable to assume that this was for when one was on horse-back as the horse reigns could be held through the loop. It was not just Scotland that imported German steel, Solingen blades were supplied all over Europe, from executioner blades to broadsword, backsword and rapier blades. Whoever Ferrara was and where ever he came from his original blades were of such fine temper that the market

---

[266] A E Mowbray (Lord Archibald Campbell) *Scottish Swords from the Battlefield at Culloden* (1971, p 34-35)
[267] Lord Archibald Campbell *Highland Dress, Arms and Ornament* (1899, p 43-51)
[268] A E Mowbray (Lord Archibald Campbell) *ibid* (1971, p 24)
[269] A V B Norman The National Trust for Scotland *Culloden The Swords and the Sorrows* (1996, p 28 plate 1:9) has a sword illustrated with the following words underneath. "The signature on the blade purports to be that of Andrea Dei Ferari, a swordsmith working in Belluno, a small town in the mountains of Venice. First recorded in 1567, he was already described as a 'talented master'. His name occurs on German blades intended for the Scottish market until the early 19th century. But very few of the blades bearing his name are early enough to be his work. The bladesmith's mark is one of the many variants used by the Wundes family of Solingen".

96

for them continued long after his death. Too own an original Ferrara sword in the 17th and 18th century was probably in modern day equivalent to having a £20,000 sports car, with a private registration.

For most Highlanders it was considered a disgrace to lose ones sword in battle, *Donnachaidh Bán Nan Orain* (fair Duncan of the songs) who fought at the battle of Falkirk lost a sword that his employer had lent him. The story goes that sometime after the battle he presented himself to his employer for his remuneration and was subsequently refused. The excuse being that he had lost the sword , no further comment is provided as to whether it was through an uncourageous act or otherwise. It could be assumed that he did act with courage since he was after all present at the battle which was not disputed. In revenge for no payment *Donnachaidh* composed a song about his experience at the battle and the owner of the sword[270].

> " *'Nuair a chruinnich iad nan ceudan,*
> *'N Iá sin air sliabh na h-Eaglais*
> *Bha ratreud air luchd na Beurla,*
> *'S ann daibh féin a b-éigin teicheadh.*
> *Ged a chaill mi anns an ám sin,*
> *Claidheamh ceanpart Chloinn-an-Leisdeir,*
> *Claidheamh bearnach a mhi-fhortain,*
> *'S ann bu choltach e ri greidlein*".

> When they gathered in their hundreds
> That day on the field of Falkirk,
> The retreat was by the English,
> It was they that had to hook it.
> I lost at that same time
> The sword of the Chief of the Clan Fletcher;
> The ugly hack sword of misfortune,
> It was no better that a gridiron.

Was the *Donnachaidh* a fox or a chicken? One will never know, but you have to give him respect for his poetic endeavors.

---

[270] J G MacKay *The Romantic Story of the Highland Garb and the Tartan* (1924, p 117)

It is estimated that one hundred and ninety swords where taken from Culloden Moor after the battle. A fence was erected using broken Jacobite swords taken from Culloden Moor; the blades were broken at the tang and the point of the blade. This atrocity was probably done by Lord Tweedale to whom they belonged to sometime after the battle. No information has been found regarding the basket hilts belong to the swords. In sheer blissful ignorance they were probably destroyed. One hundred and thirty seven blades were used to make the Twickenham fence. It's incongruous that Lord Archibald Campbell bought the fence around 1894 and proceeded to clean of the layers of paint that had protected them for so long[271]. He discovered that the vast majority were in fact made in Solingen with the famous Ferrara mark, the running wolf of Solingen and the Kings Head mark of Wundes, to name a few, see (Appendix 5). In contrast two blades were deliberately disfigured or mutilated due to their Government made connections. In Mowbray's book there is a picture of two sword blades with a Royal mark (presumably G R over a crown) disfigured probably by the act of a Jacobite[272]. The crafty Jacobite would not be stupid enough to destroy a useful weapon. These two blades were also part of the Twickenham fence. At the same time it would be incorrect to say that there were no Government troops with a Scottish blade.

The dirk or *biodag*

Particular attention has been given to the dirk because this was a weapon that arguably every mature male Highlander possessed. The origin of the Scottish dirk can be traced back to around the middle of the 16th century. One of the first recorded incidents regarding this weapon is given in the Inverness Burgh Records of 1557 (1.9). The incident recorded that Andro Dempster was the recipient of a strike to the head by Mans McGillmichell using a durcke[273]. Richard James (1592-1638) describes the weapon as a "long kind of dagger broad in

[271] Lord Archibald Campbell *Highland Dress, Arms and Ornament* (1899, p 14)
[272] A E Mowbray (Lord Archibald Campbell) *Scottish Swords from the Battlefield at Culloden* (1971, p 59)
[273] John Wallace *Scottish Swords and Dirks An illustrated reference guide to Scottish edged weapons* (1970, p,57)

the back and sharp at ye pointe which they call a durcke[274]. There are numerous other accounts of these earlier weapons and the spelling of the dirk has varied in different Burghs and Court records no doubt due to the dialect and written accounts of the time[275].

The dirks that have survived the rigors of battle and subsequent prohibitions are dated to the second half of the 17th onwards. There is also pictorial evidence of dirks illustrated in paintings from this period. The painting of a 'Highland Chieftain' by Michael Wright said to have been the 2nd Earl of Murray or (Moray) was incorrectly dated[276]. This lead to Charles Whitelaw inaccurately dating early Highland dirks, he did however pioneer the research on these weapons[277]. The painting is now dated to around the year 1660 or 1670. Previous weapons described as a dirk probably had more similarities to the earlier ballock[278] and or, dudgeon dagger. It would therefore be a fair assumption to say the dirk was first recognised towards the end of the 16th century[279].

Description of early dirks

The second half of the 17th century period of the dirks evolution has the weapon normally with a tapered blade, sharp on one side and very pointed. It is worth noting that some of these dirks have a false edge of three to six inches. The length of the blade is normally around twelve to thirteen inches, in thickness they can be from 3/16 of an inch to ½

---

[274] J T Dunbar *Orkney Record and Antiquary Society* Volume 1 (1953, p 201)

[275] John Wallace *Scottish Swords and Dirks An illustrated reference guide to Scottish edged weapons* (1970, p 57)

[276] A V B Norman *The Journal of The Arms & Armour Society, Early Military Dirks in the Scottish United Services Museum* Edinburgh Volume IV No 1 (March 1962, P 1) Refers to the 2nd Earl of Murray dated at 1660 whereas John Wallace (1970, p 58) and J T Dunbar *The Costume of Scotland* (1984, p 203) refer to the Earl of Moray dated 1660. Consensus now appears to be given on the Earls death to be dated at 1638, the painting to around 1660-1670.

[277] John Wallace *ibid* (1970, p 58)

[278] D H Caldwell *The Scottish Armoury* (1979, p 56) suggests "These early 'dirks' are possibly what we would now recognize as a ballock knives"

[279] V Dolinek & J Durdik *The encyclopedia of European Historical Weapons* (1993, p 119)

an inch. Decoration of the blade can vary from holes drilled along the back spine, blood groves and in varying degrees occasionally scrollwork. It is worth noting that what may be considered as 'decoration' nowadays arguably did serve a functional purpose. For example, the presence of blood grooves in the blade allows the weapon to be drawn out of the victim's body much easier. Since these earlier dirks were primarily stabbing weapons this appears logical. They also help in making the weapon lighter and therefore more balanced while being held in the hand. It would be fair to assume that the majority of dirks produced in the late second half of the 17th century where made from local smiths. At this time there is not much in the way of maker's marks on the blades which makes dating more imprecise. The grip at this period was made of wood such as bog oak or heather root. The grip tapered down from the pommel to the cylindrical part of the grip that was often carved with two bands of Celtic knotwork. The pommel cap itself was primarily made of brass, sometimes with concentric circle decoration; the tang nut is usually made of brass or steel. At this time no guard mounts were present where the blade fits the grip. The sheaths at this time were fairly sturdy being made from cowhide or dear skin. After the leather was stitched up the back seam it was soaked in water and then pressed with the blade inside the scabbard. This gave a stronger and firmer sheath that was shaped to the blade; generally no metal mounts were used at this time. Some weapons had a pocket at the front to accommodate a by knife which was made from wood, bone or ivory depending on the wearers financial status. The weapon was suspended from cord or leather thronging which was incorporated through holes behind the seam at the back of the sheath.

Towards the end of the 17th century we start to see broken sword blades utilised as dirk blades. This may be due to numerous factors. Wallace has suggested that the local blade smiths could not manufacture blades to the same quality and temper of imported blades that were forged in Solingen and Passau[280]. The carving on the handle has also been enhanced to cover the whole grip.

---

[280] John Wallace *Scottish Swords and Dirks An illustrated reference guide to Scottish edged weapons* (1970, p 59)

Early 18th c dirk Authors sketch

Grips made of brass, horn or bone start to be manufactured also around this time. The sheath again generally has no mounts; it is possible that the purchaser of a dirk in many cases, gentry being the exception, made the sheath himself. This would be plausible as all Highlanders were capable of tanning a hide[281] and the cutler or dirk maker often passed his work over to a separate craftsman, the sheath maker[282]. In doing this the thrifty Highlander would also save money, which was very scarce in the Highlands[283].

Macky's 1723 reference again gives a description of the dress and arms of typical Highlanders. "They have a Ponyard, Knife and fork in one sheath hanging at one side of their belt, their Pistol at the other, and their Snuff-Mill before; with a great Broadsword by their side. Their Attendance [sic] were very numerous, all in Belted Plaids, girt

---

[281] Edward Burt *Letters from a Gentleman in the North of Scotland to His Friend in London* Volume 1 (1754, p 132)

[282] C E Whitelaw *Scottish Arms Makers A biographical dictionary of makers of firearms, edged weapons and armour working in Scotland from the 15th Century to 1870* (1977, p 22)

[283] H G Graham *The Social Life of Scotland in the Eighteenth Century* (1928, p 30)

like Women's Petticoats down to the Knee; their Thighs and half of the lag bare. They had also each their Broad-sword and Ponyard"[284].

Macky's description also indicates that only the gentlemen had a knife and fork accompanying their dirk. It is worth noting that Macky refers to their sword as a 'Great broad-sword', which is carried at their side.

Burt gives a general description of what he calls 'that dangerous weapon'. "The blade is straight, and generally above a foot long, the back near an inch thick, the point goes off like a tuck, and the handle is something like that of a sickle. They pretend they can't well do without it, as being useful to them in cutting wood and upon many other occasions, but it is a concealed mischief hid under the plaid ready for secret stabbing and in a close encounter there is no defense against it"[285].

This description like many others of the 17th and 18th century is brief and does not carry much detail. It is possible that the weapons were partially hidden due to soldiers possibly being present with Burt. Soldiers were stationed at Inverness during this time therefore this is purely an assumption however; Burt also indicated that during his stay in Inverness many of the Highlanders thought of him as a spy. Burt's letters are far too descriptive in other issues of detail. No doubt if he had seen the intricate carving and beauty of these weapons he would not have described the handle as "that of a sickle"[286].

In contrast, Burt was observant enough to note that some of them (Highlanders) possess a knife called a '*Skeen-ocles*', which they conceal near the armpit. This latter weapon he refers to as being hidden and used by robbers who would do mischief with it when all think he is unarmed. Burt likely used the word robbers in a loose milieu. The portrait of Colonel Alasdair Ranaldson MacDonell of Glengarry in 1812 by Henry Raeburn is perhaps the first pictorial evidence to what is now known as a sgian dubh[287]. The skeen-ocle is

[284] John Macky *A Journey Through Scotland* (1729, p 194)
[285] Edward Burt *Letters from a Gentleman in the North of Scotland to His Friend in London* Volume 2 (1754, p 174)
[286] Edward Burt *ibid* Volume 1 (1754, p 56)
[287] F Maclean *Highlanders A History of the Highland Clans* (1995, p 226) has a good picture of MacDonell of Glengarry

probably the antecedent of the sgian dubh (black knife) named after the ebony handle adopted by the Scottish military regiments in the 19th century.

Dirk makers

Macdonald gives some intriguing information which relates to blacksmiths working in Glenlyon at an early date. McDonald's article is based on records by an earlier historian on Glenlyon called Duncan Campbell[288]. In the Glen there were five smithies' that made agricultural tools and weapons when in demand. Campbell also mentions that a family of hereditary smiths under the name of Macfarlane worked there for fourteen generations, passing on their skills from father to son in the Innerwick smithy. They were famed for being highly skilled particularly in making weapons. What is almost a certainty is that dirks were made in the vicinity. Another chronicler Alexander Stewart tells us that next to this smithy part of the stream that runs by is called 'Burn of the Dirks'; Stewart collected this information from one of the last smiths at Innerwick in 1783[289]. Many two handed swords would no doubt have been made at Innerwick. However, the name of that particular part of the stream suggests that dirks were the primary weapons for which these smiths were famed. It may be the case that only certain smiths had the prestigious honor of making these weapons. Burt mentions that smiths are in general poor, sometimes only making enough to keep them in oatmeal[290]. However, he also tells us that the finest craftsmen usually sought work for better remuneration in the Lowlands. Other famous smiths were the MacNabs of Bar Chaistealan, who where armourers to those who lived in Glen Urchay and the surrounding area. Glen Urquhart also had a family of smithies who apparently were famous for their weapons. Numerous smiths were famed for their prowess with the weapons they forged. Records also mention specific dirkmakers in and around

---

[288] D M Macdonald *Scotland's magazine and Country Life The Armourers of Glen Lyon* Volume 60 No 6 (June 1964, P 20)
[289] D M Macdonald *ibid* (1964, p 21)
[290] Edward Burt *Letters from a Gentleman in the North of Scotland to His Friend in London* Volume 1 (1754, p 128)

Perth[291] there is William Anderson admitted as a Master of his craft as durkmaker 16th February 1584. John Clerk 1593, James Wilson dirkmaker 1603 and Thomas Wilson described as a durkmaker also in 1603.

Finally, on the subject of dirks Colquhoun Grant was an officer in Col John Roy Stuart's troop. Both distinguished themselves on the field at Prestonpans in 1745. After the battle Grant pursued a party of dragoons back to Edinburgh on horseback, and "the inhabitants were amazed by the sight of the defeated cavalry galloping up the High Street followed by a single Jacobite. The Troopers just managed to get into the castle, and Colquhoun Grant, as the gate closed upon them, stuck his bloodstained dirk into it in token of defiance. He was in after life a noted W.S. in Edinburgh"[292].

The targe or shield

The highland targe is another distinctive Celtic decorated weapon used by the Highlanders. A targe was normally made from two circular pieces of wood nailed together with the grain one set across the other, normally oak or fir which was durable and strong. Pine and other soft woods debatably would have not been used because they would easily break from one or two strong blows from a sword[293]. The targe is around eighteen to twenty inches in diameter and covered with strong cowhide. On most surviving targes a central boss made from brass or silver is fixed to the middle of the targe. Some of these bosses are engraved and or pierced with heart and lozenge decoration similar to the basket hilts on highland swords. Another distinctive feature found on most surviving targes is the Celtic relief work on the leather. This normally consists of interlace work within panels equally distributed as part of the decoration. Occasionally animal or bird (zoomorphic) decoration is also included. Lower quality targes appear to lack the

[291] C E Whitelaw *Scottish Arms Makers A biographical dictionary of makers of firearms, edged weapons and armour working in Scotland from the 15th Century to 1870* (1977, p 264)
[292] A Tayler & H Tayler *Jacobite Letters to Lord Pitsligo 1745-1746* (1930, p 119)
[293] J Moran The National Trust for Scotland *Culloden The Swords and the Sorrows* (1996, p 55) Moran has suggested that pine was used in the construction of targes sometimes in combination with oak.

central boss indicating they belonged to the common clansmen. The other explanation for their lack of workmanship is that they were made in bulk to suit the immediate demands of the time. Either way there is a distinction made as to quality in the following order. Drummond[294] mentions that the paymaster for Prince Charles Laurence Oliphant of Gask ordered the following targes at Perth.

Nov 1745 To Wm Lindsay, write, for six score targes...£30 14 6
Jan 16 1746 To Wm Lindsay for 242 targets
        To 24 hydes leather from the tannage......£16 16
And for two officers targets pr order........................ £1

Edinburgh was also a place that could cope with bulk manufacture of targes and other items needed for the Highland army. Although primarily used for defence, the targe could easily be used as a weapon in conjunction with the dirk held in the same hand. One example in the Marischal Virtual Museum at the University of Aberdeen has a boss where a dirk blade can be screwed into the centre. This targe was used by Col John Roy Stuart during the 45. It was subsequently left on the eve of the Clifton skirmish along with his pistol and gilli at the stables in Lowther Hall[295]. As well as the Celtic decoration there are a vast amount of brass or silver nails forming a decorative pattern on the front of the targe. On a lot of targes these nails hold brass or silver plates, again sometimes pierced or engraved with decoration. However, this is probably a later addition to the evolution of the targe. The plates also give more protection from musket or grape shot and of course a blow from a sword or bayonet. Recent discoveries have surprisingly revealed that a musket ball will pass through a targe and probably the man behind it[296]. On the back of a targe there is a leather arm loop and a hand grip; targes that can accommodate a spike or other form of blade in the boss normally have a pocket at the back for

[294] James Drummond & Joseph Anderson *Ancient Scottish Weapons* (1881, p 17)
[295] A link is provided for the tour at
http://www.google.co.uk/Top/Regional/Europe/United_Kingdom/Scotland/Aberdeen_City_of/Arts_and_Entertainment/
[296] Dr. Tony Pollard & Neil Oliver *Two Men in a Trench II, Uncovering the secrets of British Battlefields* (2003, p 212-213)

holding the blade
or spike when not
in use. The back
of the targe is
often padded
with straw and
deerskin, hair
side out to help

Highland targe
with spike

cushion the arm from a sword or bayonet blow. There are not many
targes that have survived and of those that have, the earliest is dated to
1623[297]. Targes were not made specifically to a clan design and
Maxwell mentioned that there is a distinct lack of heraldic devices on
targes[298]. I have to agree that this is rather curious since in earlier times
the shield was one major source of identification not just on the field
of battle. However, one targe does have the badge of Lord Lovat
engraved on the brass boss with the initials AG & DG with the date
169(?)[299]. Reference has also been made to targes made from steel[300].

Scottish powder horns

During the English civil war powder holders (horns) were often
manufactured from wood, more often than not triangular in section.

[297] D H Caldwell *The Scottish Armoury* (1979, p 53)

[298] S Maxwell; T B Lindsay; C Blair; J Wallace; W Reid; J G Scott; A V B Norman
Scottish Weapons. The Scottish Art Review Magazine Volume 9 No 1 (Maxwell
1963, p 4)

[299] J Moran The National Trust for Scotland *Culloden The Swords and the Sorrows*
(1996, p 59 plate 4.12)

[300] James Drummond & Joseph Anderson *Ancient Scottish Weapons* (1881, p 14)

However, like the targe, most Scottish powder horns are decorated with beautiful Celtic ornamentation. This would consist of Highland leaf work, animals or zoomorphic and interlacing patterns. Powder horns of the early 17th onwards were made from flattened cow horn. The horn was probably immersed in very hot water for a while, the soft interior could then be removed, and then the exterior harder part of the horn was flattened when it became soft enough to take shape. The wide end of the horn was plugged with wood normally oak or fir. Fixtures or fittings were either made from pewter, lead, brass or copper, brass being the most common material used. Non ferrous metal would not give of a spark if accidently dropped or struck with another object. Fortunately, dating is more prominent on powder horns particularly to the 17th century (Appendix 4). One of the oldest dated horns is 1643 with the initials J D also inscribed. The vast differences in art work and inscriptions indicate that most surviving powder horns are of home manufacture. One could almost put this in a similar context to the scrimshaw work carried out by individuals on the whaling ships of the 19th and 20th century.

Highland pistols

The use of gunpowder in the 14th century changed battle tactics all over Europe, although only slightly at first. To begin with gunpowder was mainly used for large clumsy siege weapons. By the end of the 16th century matchlock muskets were being used by foot soldiers. The powder was ignited by a smoldering piece of cord called the match. These weapons were fairly reliable and in one style or another were used at least up to the battle of Killicrankie in 1689. Pistol makers or dagmakers were certainly plying their trade from the middle of the 16th century in Scotland. Patrick Archibald was a dagmakers who died in September 1579 in Edinburgh[301]. One distinguishing feature of Scottish pistols is that they are all of metal construction, apart from some earlier examples that have a wooden stock[302].

---

[301] C E Whitelaw *Scottish Arms Makers A biographical dictionary of makers of firearms, edged weapons and armour working in Scotland from the 15th Century to 1870* (1977, p 139)

[302] R W Latham *Antique Guns in colour 1250-1865* (1977, p 46)

Like other weapons made in the Lowlands and Highlands they possess excellence in manufacture and beauty through their distinct decoration. Again decoration consists of brass inlay work, heart and lozenge shapes foliage patterns and engraving. Scottish flintlocks fall into various categories by the shape of the butt. Flintlocks were also reliable and robust however they did have their problems. When sparks were struck from the flint there was a slight delay between the pressing of the trigger and the charge exploding, this was called 'hang fire'[303]. This could create serious problems when aiming at a moving target. The earliest is the fishtail from the late 16th century. The lemon butted pistol dates from the late 16th or early 17th century. The kidney butt style arguably a derivative of the lemon butt pistol probably of Lowland manufacture. The ramshorn style was probably the last distinctive Scottish pistol being manufactured especially in Doune. Thomas Caddell is probably the most famous Scottish pistol maker who started working in Doune around 1646. Whitelaw wrote "This famous tradesman possessed a most profound genius, and an inquisitive mind; and though a man of no education, and remote from every mean of instruction in the mechanical arts, his study and persevering exertions brought his work to so high a degree of perfection, that no pistols made in Britain excelled, or perhaps equaled those of his making, either for sureness, strength or beauty."[304] His sons carried on the family business for four generations. Other notable pistol manufacturers were Thomas Murdock of Doune Alexander Campbell also from Doune. Ramshorn pistols had a small ball and pricker between the ramshorns that curled up at the end. This could be unscrewed to clean the touch hole which could clog up with burnt powder. Another feature of these pistols is that they were not carried in a holster. The pistols had a belt hook that could be slid over a cross

---

[303] F Wilkinson *Flintlock Pistols An illustrated Reference Guide to Flintlock Pistols from the 17th to the 19th Century* (1969, p 18)
[304] C E Whitelaw *Scottish Arms Makers A biographical dictionary of makers of firearms, edged weapons and armour working in Scotland from the 15th Century to 1870* (1977, p 42)

108

belt for easy access[305]. The majority of Scottish pistols also lacked a trigger guard with the trigger being conventionally a ball shape[306].

The earliest record of a Scottish long gun (or musket) dates it to 1614 and signed 'R A' possibly made by Robert Alyson (Alison) of Dundee[307]. Most of these individual commissions were made for sporting purposes, a tinchel. Muskets were made in bulk by the likes of Thomas Grey, a dagmaker (or gunsmith) in the Canongate Edinburgh. In 1669 Grey contracted with Cuthbert Carruthers, Alexander Wilson, Hugh Somervaill, James Wilson, Adam Lawson and Francis Henderson to supply the magazine in the Castle of Edinburgh with three thousand "musquets of their own making stocked with Elme tree oiled over"[308]. Each musket was to be marked with a thistle in two locations; the price for each musket was £7.00.

The range of a musket or pistol with any degree of accuracy was approximately 60 yards. The caliber of a musket ball could between 12 and 20 millimeters, (half to three quarters of an inch) for a musket. All weapons during the 17th and 18th centuries had a smooth bore with the musket or pistol balls made from lead.

In today's society an individual is allowed to wear or carry a sgian dubh and dirk as long as it is worn with highland dress[309]. It goes without mentioning that the person should not unsheathe any weapon and brandish it about in a manner that is threatening or dangerous to other people. Re-enactors can carry muskets, flintlock pistols and other black powder weapons for educational purposes, provided they have had the necessary training and licence.

[305] J Batty The National Trust for Scotland *Culloden The Swords and the Sorrows* (1996, p 62 plate 1;22)
[306] W MacKay Junior *Some notes on Highland weapons* (1930, p 6)
[307] C E Whitelaw *Scottish Arms Makers A biographical dictionary of makers of firearms, edged weapons and armour working in Scotland from the 15th Century to 1870* (1977, p 49)
[308] C E Whitelaw *ibid* (1977, p 199-200)
[309] Offensive Weapons Act 1996 s 4 (4) (b) for educational purposes (d) as part of any national costume

Highland
flintlock
pistol
with powder
horn 18th c

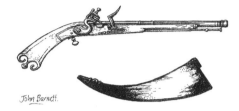

John Barnett.

Chapter VIII

Battles, and skirmishes from 1689 to 1690

Bonnie Dundee

T he first Jacobite battle was instigated by a Lowlander, John Grahame of Claverhouse who was born in 1648[310]. Bonnie Dundee was also known as Bloody Clavers and as the Highlanders called him *Iain Dubh Nan Cath* or Dark John of the Battles due to his long curled black hair. The name Bonnie Dundee was attributed to him through a poem and possibly Sir Walter Scott's song after his death.

In his youth he played chess, billiards and golf while studying at St Andrews University where he graduated in 1661. He was a handsome, charismatic and gifted man whose military experience started in 1672 volunteering for the French army. From 1674 he served with the Dutch, again as a volunteer in the Prince of Orange's own Company of Guards. During this time he served with Hugh MacKay of Scourie, a Highlander from Sutherland. At the Battle of St Nuff the Prince was dismounted from his horse and Claverhouse rescued him by carrying him off to safety on his own horse. The Prince, if he was lucky would have been taken prisoner. More than likely he would be killed outright. For this Dundee received promotion to the rank of Captain- the oldest of all military titles. Prince William did have one redeeming feature; he was a good judge of character[311]. For Bonnie Dundee serving in another country was nothing out of the ordinary and it was regarded as a kind of liberal education for a young gentleman. His first commission was commanding a newly raised troop of horse in Scotland. Dundee also fought at Drumclog, Bothwell Bridge and various other skirmishes against the Covenanters. In 1682 he was promoted to the rank of Colonel with his own regiment of horse. In

---

[310] J MacLehose *Scottish History & Life* (Brook, 1902, p 126) many great Scots were Lowlanders for example William Wallace, Robert Bruce and Robert Burns.
[311] Sir Charles Petrie *The Stuarts* 2nd edition. (1958, p 251)

1686 he was again promoted to a Major General having command of all his "Majesty's [Horse] Forces in Scotland"[312] where he suppressed Lowland Covenanters in Dumfries and Galloway. Two years later he received his Peerage as Viscount Dundee and Lord Grahame of Claverhouse from King James VII.

The build up to the battle

William of Orange who was James VII and II nephew was voted to take over as King at the Convention Parliament in Edinburgh on the 4th April 1689. James VII had little support at the Convention. Bonnie Dundee and some staunch followers of James VII left Edinburgh with fifty men to start the first Jacobite rising. Around the 16th of April 1689 Lord Dundee raised the Jacobite standard. Later on a sum, of £20,000 was put on the head of Dundee; but his men still faithful to the cause would not betray him. This is another display of loyalty evident throughout the Jacobite campaigns. At Inverness Dundee did not receive much support. Therefore he made his way to Stratherick then to *Chille Chuimein* now known as Fort Augustus. Two days later he marched rapidly to Dunkeld then Perth where he obtained taxes and arms that were intended for the Government troops.

General Hugh MacKay of Scourie (1640-1692), a brave and pious man had been commissioned to crush Dundee. MacKay, like Dundee, had vast military experience having served in France, Crete and Holland. On the 26th of May MacKay left David Ross of Balnagown in charge of around five hundred men at Inverness[313].

Dundee marched west to the Lochaber area sending out the fiery cross to rally more men which he received. Dundee, despite being a Lowlander had the reverence from all who followed him. This extended to the point where MacDonald of Keppoch begged his forgiveness for a misdemeanour. "He pleaded in excuse that he had burnt Dunachton in belief that Mackintosh had recently declared for General Mackay; but, since he had been wrong in this, he could but promise greater caution in the future. And finally he swore that neither

[312] M Barrington *Grahame of Claverhouse Viscount Dundee* (1911, p 382)
[313] B Robertson *Jacobite Activities in and around Inverness 1688-1746* (1925, p 3)

he nor any of his men should henceforth start hostilities without Dundee's express command"[314].

Both armies harassed each other and at one point MacKay intercepted a messenger from his army with intelligences for Dundee. Lieutenant-Colonel William Livingston, Captain Alexander Bruce, and three other Captains were sent down to Edinburgh as conspirators. MacKay also recommended that they be tortured[315].

On June 9th MacKay heard that Dundee was ill and was camped near Abernethy woods. MacKay had caught a few of Dundee's stragglers previously so he thought Dundee's army was demoralized. He sent a detachment of two hundred horse and dragoons under the command of Sir Thomas Livingston[316], his main force he kept as support. At the same time the MacLean's of Duart around two hundred in number were on their way to support Dundee. Both parties noticed each other from afar near the Spey. However, Hector MacLean of Lochbuie at first thought it was Dundee's army then he spotted the red coats and took advantage. Using the terrain the MacLean's ran up a hill called Knockbrecht at the same time they dislodged boulders to fall down on the red coats. The dragoons ran up the hill in pursuit and the MacLean's charged downhill and was victorious. Some of the dragoons were Scots who changed sides and helped towards the encouraging victory. Both sides eventually came to a full scale battle at the pass of Killicrankie.

The battle of Killicrankie (27th July 1689)

It is estimated that there was around two thousand five hundred men on Dundee's side; MacKay had a force of around five thousand men. Before the initial battle snipers fired from a small cottage half way up the hill on MacKay's men whilst making their way through the

---

[314] M Barrington *Grahame of Claverhouse Viscount Dundee* (1911, p 287)
[315] M Barrington *ibid* (1911, p 291) Bishop Burnett asserted that "General MacKay's humanity was so excessive as to make him scarcely fit for military command"
[316] D Love *Jacobite Stories* (2007, p 7) has obviously got confused between Sir Thomas Livingston who became the Lord Advocate for Scotland and Lieutenant-Colonel William Livingston. He cites Sir Thomas as one of the conspirators who were sent to Edinburgh. Love also mentions that Sir Thomas was killed at the Spey fracas.

pass. Evidence of snipers and light hand to hand fighting has also been recently confirmed around this area by Pollard and Oliver[317]. This tactic employed by Dundee would unravel and help dishearten the Government troops which consisted of "English dragoons, three Scots Brigades from Holland, and militia raised by levy"[318]. To Mackay's detriment most of his army was composed of new recruits that had never been in battle before. Dundee on the other hand had trained his forces well. The tactic of the Highlanders was to charge and then within a distance of twenty yards or so, fire their muskets or pistols, drop them, and continue through the pistol and musket smoke shouting their battle cries to complete the devastating charge into the enemy. Highlanders where all too familiar with their terrain and used it to their advantage and if at all possible would make the charge downhill. On the 27th of July 1689 the Highlanders, some Lowlanders and a contingent of around three hundred Irish[319] commanded under Bonnie Dundee fired their muskets and pistols then charged at the enemy armed with pistol, dirk, target and their dreaded claidheamh mòr's. The Highlanders charge scattered the ranks of General MacKay's army despite MacKay having twice the firepower approximately five thousand men and soon all who could ran for their lives. Pollard and Oliver's recent work on the battle site has confirmed that the Government musketry only managed two or three volleys of fire due to the high and low points of ground were the Jacobite forces charged[320]. The two handed swords and broadswords had such devastating effect that decapitated bodies and pieces of limbs were strewn over the pass[321].

Many of MacKay's men probably drowned through soldiers climbing over their injured comrades to cross the river Garry. The carnage of the battle lasted approximately five minutes and it is estimated that over two thousand of MacKay's men fell at the hands of the Highlanders muskets, swords, dirks and other weapons. One

[317] Dr. Tony Pollard & Neil Oliver *Two Men in a Trench II, Uncovering the secrets of British Battlefields* (2003, p 230)
[318] W H Murray *Rob Roy MacGregor His life and Times* (1982, p 78)
[319] B Robertson *Jacobite Activities in and around Inverness 1688-1746* (1925, p 5)
[320] Dr. Tony Pollard & Neil Oliver *Two Men in a Trench II, Uncovering the secrets of British Battlefields* (2003, p 234)
[321] W H Murray *ibid* (1982, p 88)

Government soldier by the name Donald McBane wrote later on that he jumped a span of eighteen feet or so over the Gorge in his escape[322]. This part of the Gorge is now known as the Soldiers leap.

It is a fair argument that MacKay lost the battle partly due to large gaps in his line and new raw recruits. The Highlanders covered ground very quickly, after firing their musket or pistols. The new ring bayonet had not been used in Scotland before[323] and MacKay's men after firing had to insert their awkward plug bayonet into the muzzle of their musket. This took time and many of his men panicked the resulting weapon was not that effective either against the well-armed Highlanders on this occasion. It has also been recently discovered that MacKay's men had a form of grenade which they flung at the highlanders in a last second panic, apparently without much effect[324].

Despite victory, Dundee received a mortal wound near the end of the battle whilst charging down the centre of the hill to encourage his men. Burt mentioned that there was a great stone raised on the spot where Dundee fell[325]. He lived for a few hours after the battle knowing that he had done his duty for his King, obviously meaning King James. Between six hundred and nine hundred Highlanders fell[326] most falling from the initial firepower during the charge. Many great men died in the battle, clan Cameron, and clan Donald had many clansmen slain amongst other clans. Young Glengarry's son Donald accounted for eighteen of the enemy before he himself was struck down[327]. MacKay fled to Stirling where he regrouped his men. He then made his way to Perth. His losses were far more catastrophic, with over two thousand men.

---

[322] M Rector *Highland Swordsmanship* (2001, p 26) from D McBane *The Expert Sword-man's Companion* (1728)

[323] H Brown *A Short History of Scotland* (1951, p 280)

[324] Dr. Tony Pollard & Neil Oliver *Two Men in a Trench II, Uncovering the secrets of British Battlefields* (2003, p 234-235)

[325] Edward Burt *Letters from a Gentleman in the North of Scotland to His Friend in London* Volume 2 (1754, p 225)

[326] J Prebble *The Lion in the North* (1981, p 278) states that 600 Highlanders were killed; M Barrington *Grahame of Claverhouse Viscount Dundee* (1911, p 355) mentions that the figure was nearer 900 according to an indecisive letter Dundee wrote before his death.

[327] M Barrington *Grahame of Claverhouse Viscount Dundee* (1911, p 367)

Dundee's most serious wound was in the lower part of his left side and MacKay claimed his regiment had fired the fatal shot. However, his regiment was one of the first to beat a retreat in anticipation of the pursuing Highlanders once they had broken through MacKay's lines. In Barrington's words "The victory was complete. The Baggage, tents, provisions, and artillery of General MacKay were at the disposal of the Highlanders; amongst their trophies was the Orange Standard carried by MacKay's own regiment"[328]. Many of the Highlanders subsequently left the Pass of Killicrankie demoralized by Dundee's death. Others made there way home with the spoils of war while some made their way to Dunkeld.

Dundee's body was wrapped in two plaids and buried at St Brides Church at Old Blair. Dundee was rumored to be the Grand Master of a Jacobite Templar movement in the Montrose area. On removing his breast plate the Templar cross was said to have been worn by Dundee. John Erskine (Earl of Mar) was also rumored to be the next Grand Master of the order after Dundee's death. However, Mar would only have been fourteen years of age at the time; the confusion may be through Mar inheriting his title also in 1689.

Legends are quick on the uptake and it was rumored later that Dundee was killed by a silver button used in place of a musket ball. The Covenanters who hated Dundee with a vengeance believed that he was in league with the devil himself.

One Edinburgh contemporary wrote of Dundee a few weeks after his death[329].

> *"O last and best of Scots, who didst maintain*
> *Thy country's freedom from a foreign reign,*
> *New people fill the land now thou art gone,*
> *New Gods the temples, and new King's the throne,*
> *Scotland and thou didst in each other live,*
> *Nor would'st thou her nor could she thee survive,*
> *Farewell, who dying didst support the State,*
> *And could not fall but with thy country's fate"*

---

[328] M Barrington *Grahame of Claverhouse Viscount Dundee* (1911, p 367)
[329] M Barrington *ibid* (1911, p 375)

It was not too long after the battle that MacKay claimed to have invented the ring bayonet. This was portentous because the French where using a similar type of ring bayonet as far back as 1678. The French are reputed to have invented the ring bayonet in 1671 and that the term 'bayonet' was derived from these weapons being first made in Bayonne[330].

MacKay was however instrumental in Fort William being built as a strong hold since it had a strong strategic position. He later fought at Aughrim in Ireland against the Jacobites but was killed at the battle of Steinkirk in 1692.

The siege of Dunkeld (21st of August 1689)

On the 21st of August the Highlanders between three and four thousand strong again with other clans joining the army approached Dunkeld. The Burgh of Dunkeld was held by the Earl of Angus's Regiment or as they were better known as the Cameronians[331], of whom there were only twelve hundred men under the leadership of Lieutenant Colonel William Cleland[332]. He was a young man with military experience having fought at Bothwell Bridge and against Dundee at Drumclog in 1679. Unlike MacKay he had the ability to galvanize his men. This time the Highlanders were under the command of Colonel Alexander Cannon who was an Irish officer [333] and Dundee's successor. His leadership skills were however impaired by his continual drinking bouts with Lord Dunfermline. This time the tables were turned. The Cameronians were more resilient to Cannons onslaught. For hours on end the brave Cameronians held the fire stricken streets of Dunkeld from the Highlanders. At one point the Cameronians had to strip lead from the roof of the Cathedral to make makeshift musket balls[334]. Cleland ironically shared the same fate of

---

[330] Francis Grose *Military Antiquities Respecting A History of the English Army* Volume 1 (1801, p 162)

[331] The Cameronians were named after Reverend Richard Cameron who had fought on the side of the Covenanters and who was killed in 1680.

[332] H Brown *A Short History of Scotland* (1951, p 280)

[333] T Thompson *A History of the Scottish People* " Mackay's Memoirs; Dundee's Memoires; Balcarras" (1894, p 222)

[334] H Brown *ibid* (1951, p 280)

Dundee, being victorious in Battle and falling in the last hour or battle[335]. Prebble mentions that Cleland was killed in the first hour of the assault with a musket or pistol shot to the liver and head[336]. Cleland's victory was however more complete with the death of around three hundred highlanders. With no real plan of action the intractable Highland army gave up and made there way off to the hills, some homeward bound to lick there wounds.

The rout of Cromdale (1st May 1690)

The rest of the Highland army kept themselves to the north of Scotland with no strong leadership and no real plans of what to do next. Sir Ewan Cameron assumed control of those that were left and a council was held with other chiefs who were present. They appealed to King James VII for more support; but he had similar troubles in Ireland. He did however send arms and clothing with a few officers and a commission for Major-General Buchan to take command as Commander-in-Chief in Scotland[337]. Another council of was held with the agreement to postpone a full mustering of the clans till better weather came. However, it was agreed that Buchan detach himself with twelve hundred men to weaken defenses in the Lowlands. Buchan marched down the Spey to Cromdale. Numbers were still diminishing and by the 1st May 1690 those that were left, some eight hundred men were camped at Cromdale. The Highland Chiefs and officers had warned Buchan against this decision but like so many other forthcoming leaders he was too head strong to listen to their advice.
Meanwhile Sir Thomas Livingston who was in charge of the Garrison at Inverness made a surprise attack on the Highlanders. Luckily, there were no sentries posted for watch and there was no reconnaissance of the area carried out by the Jacobites either[338] all because of Buchan's inept leadership. The Jacobites were asleep and outnumbered but fortunately a mist came down enabling an escape route to be taken. Approximately three hundred Highlanders were

---

[335] B Lenman *The Jacobite Cause* (1986, p 29)
[336] J Prebble *The Lion in the North* (1981, p 278)
[337] B Robertson *Jacobite Activities in and around Inverness 1688-1746* (1925, p 5)
[338] W H Murray *Rob Roy MacGregor His life and Times* (1982, p 93)

killed with around one hundred taken as prisoners. Livingston's men pursued a group of Jacobites, around a hundred who presumably got detached, lost in the fog. Another conflict ensued on Granish moor where most of the Jacobites were killed.

Not long after this James was defeated by the Prince of Orange at the Battle of the Boyne in 1690. James subsequently went over to France in exile. Buchan also escaped to France later to fight for the cause at Sheriffmuir in 1715.

Chapter IX

The massacre of Glencoe (13th November 1692)

After the Battle of Killiecrankie and the Battle of the Boyne the Government was terrified that another rising would occur. Their first plan of action as always was a bribe, amounting to £20,000 to be distributed amongst the chiefs for their allegiance to William III[339]. The Williamite clans where more than happy to accept the bribe, or if the truth be told, their chiefs where. Chiefs with no allegiance would always refuse the money. This made the Jacobite clans even more resentful of the Government. The Governments next step was to enforce an oath of allegiance by the 1st of January 1692. Sir Thomas Livingston the new Lord Advocate for Scotland and John Dalrymple the Master of Stair were instrumental in the construction of the plan. Those who did not take the oath by this date were to be proclaimed and treated as outlaws[340].

At the time of the massacre Robert Campbell of Glenlyon (1630-1696) was sixty years of age. He had only just received his commission as a Captain in the Earl of Argyles Regiment at the age of fifty nine[341]. He was a self-indulgent man who was a compulsive gambler and a heavy drinker. The only property he had left was the family estate in Glenlyon. This property was in his wife's name which is probably the only reason they still had the property. He was in serious debt to his neighbours and his clansmen, indeed anyone who would lend him money. Glenlyon was always at the centre of clan war fair between the Campbells and MacDonalds. One skirmish that took place resulted in thirty six MacDonalds being hanged by Mad Colin of Glenlyon. Mad Colin as he was commonly known was the great grandfather of Robert Campbell. Irreverently, the MacDonalds killed the same number of Campbells just after a Campbell wedding in

---

[339] C W Thomson *Scotland's Work and Worth*. Volume 1 (1909, p 253) mentions "The Earl of Breadlbane had been allowed a sum of £20,000 in 1690 with which to bribe various chiefs into submit ion"

[340] H Brown *A Short History of Scotland* (1951, p 282)

[341] J Prebble *Glencoe* (1973, p 185)

Glenlyon in 1646. After the battle of Dunkeld (1689) some of the MacDonalds also looted Glenlyon. With Robert Campbell's financial desperation and his previous clan feuds with the MacDonald's he was the ideal person for this commission.

The Glencoe MacDonald's amongst other clans, in truth were irredeemable freebooters with MacIan the Clan Chieftain being a fairly stubborn but proud man who waited till the last possible moment to give his clans allegiance to William III. MacIan had met with the Earl of Breadlbane and other chiefs earlier in 1691 to discuss their submission and the promise of a pardon on taking the oath of allegiance; MacIan was one of the chiefs who also reluctantly agreed. Clan Henderson also lived in Glencoe for many generations before the MacDonald's, and MacIan's piper was a Henderson. Campbell and the Militia force were deceitful from the very start convincing MacIan that they were in the vicinity to collect taxes. The sole reason for their visit was to obtain suitable quarters and they were there as friends. The chiefs' younger son Alexander Macdonald was married to Glenlyon's niece, the sister of Rob Roy.

The following passage is taken from a re-print of a contemporary account of the massacre originally written in 1692[342]. "MacIan, the Chief of the MacDonald's of Glen Coe, through an error was too late [in taking the oath], yet he obtained a written pardon. It is said- though it has been denied- that the fact of his having taken the oath of allegiance was suppressed by Sir John Dalrymple, afterwards Earl of Stair. Be this as it may, the King's signature was obtained to an order directing the Commander of the Forces to extirpate that set of thieves, the MacDonald's. On the 1st of February 1692, 120 soldiers, mostly Campbell's, the hereditary enemies of the MacDonald's, entered Glen Coe under the command of Lieutenant Robert Campbell of Glen Lyon. They were quartered on the Inhabitants, with whom they dwelt under a false show of friendship for twelve days. The morning of the 13th had been fixed for the massacre, but owing to Lieutenant-Colonel Hamilton having failed to occupy the passes about 300 men and women escaped, to die, however, in most cases, from cold and hunger.

---

[342] E Goldsmid *The Massacre of Glencoe 13th of February 1692 Being A Reprint of that a Contemporary Account of that Ruthless Butchery* (1885, p 6-7)

Thirty eight men, women and children were butchered in cold blood, their huts burnt to the ground, and their flocks driven away." Extirpate means to 'root out' or 'destroy' draconian measures to say the least, even in the late 17th century. The account also mentioned that two of MacIan's sons escaped the massacre only because they had overheard two soldiers discussing the matter not more than fifteen minutes before the orders were to be carried out[343]. Upon hearing the conversation MacIan's sons went around the huts that were not so closely guarded informing those inside what was about to happen thus enabling them to make good their escape. Glenlyon's soldiers started the slaughter at five am killing men, women and children who had no weapons at hand and who had provided the customary highland hospitality with great kindness as best they could for the previous twelve days. MacIan was shot in the head while trying to put his breeches on. One other officer who shared rank with Glenlyon was present, Thomas Drummond, a ruthless uncompassionate man who killed a twelve year old boy clinging to Glenlyons legs begging for mercy[344]. MacDonald's and no doubt Henderson's were shot, bayoneted with some just simply being bludgeoned to death with the butt of a musket. Others were burnt alive and some were bound hand and foot, flung on dung heaps and shot dead[345]. After the carnage the soldiers began looting from the half naked, dead bodies and empty huts that had not been burnt to the ground. Two soldiers did refuse to carry out their orders and subsequently they were put in a Glasgow prison.

After the massacre Glenlyon was heard to be bragging in coffee houses in Edinburgh that he would do it again if need be. "Nay Glen lyon is so far from denying it, that he brags of it , and justifies the Action publicly: He said in the Royal Coffee-House in Edinburgh, that he would do it again; nay, That he would stab any man in Scotland or in England, without asking the cause, if the King gave him Orders, and that it was every good Subjects duty to do so; and I am credibly informed that Glen lyon and the rest of them have addressed the

---

[343] E Goldsmid *The Massacre of Glencoe 13th of February 1692 Being A Reprint of that a Contemporary Account of that Ruthless Butchery* (1885, p 23)
[344] R R McIan *Costumes of the Clans of Scotland* (1845, p 216-217)
[345] J Prebble *Glencoe* (1973, p 213)

Council for a reward for their good service, in destroying Glencoe, pursuant to their Orders" [346]. Coffee Houses in Edinburgh also sold ale and other liquors' associated with the taverns or alehouses of Scotland at the time[347]. The name was more than likely adopted to suit the fashionable trends in London.

It must be pointed out that the blame does not just lie on Glenlyon's shoulders. Sir John Dalrymple the Master of Stair who was the Secretary of State for Scotland gave out the orders. He had expected "an utter annihilation of the Clan" with a stronger Government force stopping any stragglers leaving the Glen who did not arrive in time due to the weather[348]. It was also Dalrymple who asked William to sign the papers and make an example of MacIan's clan. He also conveniently forgot to inform William that MacIan had taken the oath even though it was only a few days late[349]. All in all, thirty eight men, women and children were slaughtered with approximately three hundred others dying as a direct result of Dalrymple's orders along with Glenlyon and Drummonds hatred for the MacDonald's. "Within two weeks news of the massacre was out and a pamphlet by Charles Lesley, an Irishman, turned the event into national scandal"[350]. There was even some disbelief in England, then public outcry north and south of the Border that the massacre did in fact take place. This highlighted all the atrocities that happened so an inquiry was made by the Scottish Parliament in 1695[351]. True there had been other massacres of a similar nature but this was "murder under trust, planed and ordered by the Kings servants"[352], or murder without objection (*nemine contradicente*) which was abhorrent in the Highlands and I should add anywhere else. Dalrymple was forced out of office into retirement with a full pardon and a pension from William. He was a shunned man. By then Glenlyon and his subalterns were serving in Flanders and the

---

[346] E Goldsmid *The Massacre of Glencoe 13th of February 1692 Being A Reprint of that a Contemporary Account of that Ruthless Butchery* (1885, p 26)

[347] M W Stuart *Old Edinburgh Taverns* (1952, p 166) James Row established the first Coffee House in Edinburgh in 1673 at Robertson Land in Parliament Close.

[348] C W Thomson *Scotland's Work and Worth* Volume 1 (1909, p 254)

[349] H Brown *A Short History of Scotland* (1951, p 282)

[350] http://www.contemplator.com/history/glencoe.html#top

[351] E Goldsmid *ibid* (1885, p 71-74)

[352] J Prebble *Glencoe* (1973, p 282)

onus was on William to have them brought back to face justice. This never happened, William had also signed the papers, later denying that he had understood the content i.e., "extirpate that set of thieves" and therefore he obviously was never going to accept any blame either.

As a matter of interest George Mackenzie (1639-1691) who was a distinguished lawyer refused the position of Lord Advocate for Scotland which he had previously held. The position was offered on the condition that he did not prosecute those involved in the Glencoe massacre. Mackenzie wrote a very influential work *"Institutions of the Law of Scotland"* first published in 1684[353]. Mackenzie also founded the library of the Faculty of Advocates in Edinburgh in 1689.

Campbell of Glenlyon, as one would suspect died in poverty in Bruges in 1696, far away from the country and Highlanders he so much despised.

Glencoe is approximately ten miles long and visitors are drawn by the beautiful scenery, its climbing attributes and its historical connections. There's a stone in a field at Garnock near Glencoe called Henderson's stone and this is where the Henderson's, who were hereditary pipers to the MacDonald's used to play their pipes back in the 17th century. No one could pass through or stay in Glencoe without giving thought to what happened on that fateful day so many years ago.

A Massacre is the correct description of what happened on the 13th of February 1692 in Glencoe. I have to rebut any account that indicates it was not a massacre and I am sure most readers on the subject would agree[354].

---

[353] R T Skinner *The Royal Mile* (1947, p 103)

[354] During the course of my research I discovered that some websites made ridiculous pretensions with regard to certain facts on the Massacre at Glencoe. Such as "The truth about the **Glencoe Massacre** has not really been told properly" and **"The Massacre of Glencoe** was not a true Massacre" lastly and this one sticks in my throat "The **Glencoe Massacre** is a good story for tourists" totally irrational statements. However, I can only comment further in stating that websites should be treated with caution regarding the reliability of the information they provide. http://www.bayviewkentallen.co.uk/glencoemassacre.html

Chapter X

Battles from 1700 to 1719

The French Jacobite retreat (13th March 1708)

Although no actual battle was fought it was an important event that displayed the force of Jacobite sympathy from France. The highlanders in general were still cautious with regards to the Whig Government. With the massacre of Glencoe still fresh in a lot of Jacobite minds, they had done everything to prevent the Union in 1707, but to no avail. This Union also had the effect of cutting off any of King James's heirs to the throne. In 1708 a plot was hatched by Colonel Nathanial Hooke an Irishman and the notorious Simon Fraser (Master of Lovat at the time)[355]. Hook was employed by the French Government as an agent between the Jacobite supporters in Scotland[356]. Hook and Fraser both with vast experience in the activities of secret mediation turned to the French King Louis XIV for assistance to help put James's son on his father's throne. Louis XIV had also proclaimed James VIII and III as the new King on the death of his father James VII and II in 1701[357]. Claude Forbin Comte de (1656-1733) was given the Commission which he accepted with reluctance. From the conception of the expedition to the end of it, Forbin believed the whole enterprise was doomed to failure. On 6TH March 1708 Louis sent Admiral Forbin with a fleet of five ships and twenty one frigates with some four thousand French troops[358] including the nineteen year old James Edward Stuart to Scotland. The plan was to restore James to one realm, Scotland[359]. With the unpopular Union it was hoped most Scot's would want "the restoration

---

[355] B Lenman *The Jacobite Cause* (1986, p 41)
[356] C S Stevenson *Inglorious Rebellion The Jacobite Risings of 1708, 1717 and 1719* (1973, p 65)
[357] C W Thomson *Scotland's Work and Worth* Volume 1 (1909, p 259)
[358] H Brown *A Short History of Scotland* (1951, p 291)
[359] B Lenman *ibid* (1986, p 41)

of James's son"[360]. The town of Edinburgh was in a state of joy with James's loyal subjects awaiting his arrival. The Government forces who occupied Stirling and Edinburgh castle had little or, no powder or ammunition. The restoration would give Scotland and France more negotiating power over England. The voyage was not without tribulations and they were forced to alter course to try and avoid gales. The fleet sought shelter at Ostend dunes where three ships the *Porteus, Guerrier* and the *Barrentin* were nearly lost after breaking their cables. During this time of distress Forbin openly mocked those suffering from sea-sickness "I can do nothing, the wine is drawn and you must drink it. Suffer, feel as uncomfortable as you please; I'm quite content, and don't pity you at all" was his gloating reaction[361]. At last the weather calmed and the fleet once more set sail. The English however, had their spies and a fleet was sent to counter attack the French fleet under the command of Sir George Byng. The twenty eight English men-of -war entered the Firth and stopped the French fleet from landing. The French being no Military match made haste their escape fleeing northward[362] to regroup off the Aberdeenshire coast. However, one French ship was captured, the *Salisbury* with Lord Griffin and the crew on board. Lord Griffin was condemned to death but received a reprieve only to die two years later in the Tower. Nineteen year old James had requested to be let ashore near Fife, Montrose or indeed anywhere but he was ignored. It could be fair to assume that Forbin used James's wellbeing as an excuse not to anchor on the shores of Scotland. Inevitably some Jacobites believed that Forbin had no intention to land at all.

The 1715 rising

On August 30th 1713 Louis XIV died and James's restoration had an ascetic outlook from the French[363].The peace Treaty of Utrecht

---

[360] H Brown *A Short History of Scotland* (1951, p 291)
[361] C S Stevenson *Inglorious Rebellion The Jacobite Risings of 1708, 1717 and 1719* (1973, p 70)
[362] J Prebble *Glencoe* (1973, p 297)
[363] R E Hutchison National Galleries of Scotland *The Jacobite Rising of 1715* (1965, p 12)

required that the Regent Orléans who ruled over France after Louis death recognize the Protestant succession to the throne of Great Britain. A provision in the Treaty also recognized Philip, Louis grandson as King of Spain. James VIII and III had to move out of France, taking residence at the independent Duchy of Lorraine[364]. However, before Louis death he wrote a letter to Philip V of Spain and obtained financial assistance for the Jacobite cause. James and Philip signed an agreement to this effect but there were two catches. The first, in the event of a restoration James would support Spain on their claims although territorial, in Italy. The second Great Britain would be a fully Catholic nation.

There was even more disappointment with the Union and many Scot's rightly so, thought Articles where prejudice in England's favor[365] or they were being broken. On the 1st August 1714 Queen Anne died without surviving issue. In accordance with the Act of Settlement Sophie of Hanover's son German George was given the throne of Great Britain since Sophie had also died in 1714. George had nothing but contempt for all things English[366]. He could hardly speak a word of English to boot. After Anne's death, the Jacobites where hoping that the restoration of James would happen, but it never came.

Almost one year after Queen Anne's death, John Erskine the Earl of Mar (1675-1732) lost his position as Secretary of State to Scotland and fell out of esteem with George I. Mar was given the nickname Bobbing John for the way he changed his political allegiance. The Earl of Mar foreseeing no real future for himself made his move. Mar left London and proceeded to Scotland disguised as a workman on a coal sloop which sailed to Fife. He was accompanied by Major General Hamilton, Colonel John Grey and a few trustworthy servants. Mar then proceeded to Aberdeenshire to rouse the Scottish Jacobites. On the 20th August Mar invited various noblemen and clan chiefs under the pretence of a tinchel[367] or hunting party to be held at Aboyne. Every year in August this important event attracted nobles and gentlemen

---

[364] B Lenman *The Jacobite Cause* (1986, p 44)
[365] H Brown *A Short History of Scotland* (1951, p 290)
[366] H Kemp *The Jacobite Rebellion* (1975, p 9)
[367] A Warrack *The Scots Dialect Dictionary* (1988, p 615) defines a tinchel as "a circle formed by sportsmen to encircle deer".

with their respective servants from all over Scotland. Some Nobel men who attended were the Marques of Huntly, the Duke of Gordon's eldest son, the Marques of Tullibardine, the Earls of Nithsdale, Marischal, Traquair, Errol, Southesk, Carnwath, Seaforth and Linlithgow; Viscounts Kilsyth, Kenmure, Kingston and Stormont, Lords Drummond and Rollo[368]. On the 26th the tinchel was held with great feasting and raised glasses. Mar delivered a rousing speech to those present announcing himself as major general of the Scottish army. However, this was only done in anticipation of the forthcoming commission that was not dated till the 7th September[369]. On the 6th September 1715 Mar raised the standard for the Jacobite restoration at Castleton of Braemar[370]. Figures are vague as to how many were present but there were possibly six hundred; propaganda on the other hand said only sixty were present. When the Scottish standard was raised the golden ball on top of the flag pole fell off. This was a bad omen for the superstitious Highlanders and this led to lack of enthusiasm at the start of the rising. Meanwhile, the English Jacobites had been prevented from rising by the arrest of their ring leaders in the south-west of England. Mar had raised around ten thousand men after calling all good men to fight "for the relief of our country from oppression and a foreign yoke too heavy for us ... to bear"[371]. The Earl of Mar seized Perth on the 14th of September with a detachment of forces and Brigadier William Macintosh of Borlum seized Inverness. Mar arrived in the Perth camp on the 28th September and Sinclair noted that discipline was severely lacking through the whole chain of command. Mar soon realized that funds were needed for food, powder and ammunition therefore he reintroduced an old land tax. Sinclair pointed out that Mar consulted no one even on major decisions and he believed without a doubt that Mar pocketed a large amount of the raised funds[372].

---

[368] R E Hutchison National Galleries of Scotland *The Jacobite Rising of 1715* (1965, p 14)

[369] C S Stevenson *Inglorious Rebellion The Jacobite Risings of 1708, 1717 and 1719* (1973, p 114)

[370] H Brown *A Short History of Scotland* (1951, p 294)

[371] W Moffat *A History of Scotland*, book 4 (1985, p 25)

[372] C S Stevenson *ibid* (1973, p 126-129)

At Inverness Borlum soon found out that arms were held at Culloden House therefore he marched forth to obtain them. However, the Lady of the House Mrs. Forbes learned of Borlum's intentions therefore she hid the arms in a safe place. It must be said that when Borlum approached the House Mrs. Forbes defied him and told him to do his worst[373]. Abandoning the idea Borlum decided to leave for Perth to regroup with Mar at Perth.

Sinclair also heard through a family friend or spy that there was a small ship with ammunition and powder near the port of Leith, in fact the ship was off Burntisland. The arms, some three thousand in total were destined for Lord Sutherland who was in the Hanoverian army. Sinclair immediately informed Mar who was indecisive how many men should go with Sinclair. Eventually they came to an agreement and Sinclair set off for Burntisland. They did manage to obtain the arms from the ship and the Town Guard but it came to approximately three hundred arms. This was a big disappointment for Sinclair but debatably still successful from a moral building perspective.

Meanwhile the Government appointed John Campbell the Duke of Argyle, chief of clan Campbell (1673-1743), who had vast experience in warfare to lead the Hanoverian army[374]. At thirty seven years old he had over twenty one years of military experience, distinguishing himself on several occasions. Argyle was supported by the Sutherland chief, the MacKay's, Munroe's, Ross's, The Laird of Grant and his followers in Strathspey and of course Forbes of Culloden,[375] and later by the notorious Simon Master of Lovat in the north, arguably through necessity. Three regiments of foot were brought back from Ireland arriving in Edinburgh on the 24th August. Major General Wightman stationed troops at Stirling castle and at the bridge over the forth. Hopefully, this would stop Mar proceeding south in any great numbers.

---

[373] B Robertson *Jacobite Activities in and around Inverness 1688-1746* (1925, p 7)
[374] B Lenman *The Jacobite Cause* (1986, p 46)
[375] B Robertson *ibid* (1925, p 6)

The siege at Preston (12th November 1715)

On the 9th of October Mar redeployed part of his army, two thousand men under the command of Brigadier William Macintosh of Borlum, ordering them to take Edinburgh Castle. Prebble mentions that "Macintosh of Borlum was a middle-aged but redoubtable soldier who should more properly have commanded the whole enterprise"[376]. There were military stores and £60,000 in gold still left over from the money paid to Scotland from the Treaty of Union[377]. Argyle, through anticipation and intelligence from one of his spies sent two hundred infantry and three hundred dragoons to enter by the West Port and to hold Edinburgh. Borlum arrived at Jock's Lodge approximately a mile from the city and soon realized Argyle had won the race. A previous attempt had been made to take the castle by Drummond of Balhaldie on the 8th September[378]. Edinburgh Jacobites some whom were students and lawyers[379] gave assistance but there attempt failed. Three guards were bribed but one of them had a loose tongue. A few shots were fired and four of the Jacobites were caught. Later it was discovered that the ladders used to scale the walls were far from long enough, disastrous planning from the very start. Borlum did not have a fighting force large enough to take Edinburgh. Therefore he marched down to the Fort of Leith. The fort was partly in ruin but it was still a formidable strong hold for the Jacobites[380]. In Leith Borlum ransacked the Customs Houses and released forty Jacobites who had previously been captured crossing the Forth. Later word was received that a rebellion had broken out in Dumfriesshire and Northumberland. Borlum marched to support them occupying Seton Palace to the east of Edinburgh for a few days before departing to the borders[381]. At Kelso he was joined by the Lowland Jacobites under the command of Viscount Kenmure and the Earl of Nithsdale. On approaching England four hundred Highlanders deserted making their way back north, most

---

[376] J Prebble *Glencoe* (1973, p 282)
[377] R E Hutchison *The Jacobite Rising of 1715* (1965, p 18)
[378] L Weirter *The story of Edinburgh Castle* (1913, p 152-153)
[379] L Weirter *ibid* (1913 p 152-153)
[380] R Mackie *A Short History of Scotland* (1947, p 346)
[381] H Brown *A Short History of Scotland* (1951, p 295)

of who were captured[382]. Thomas Forster also joined with a small
force from Northumberland. With around three thousand men in total
they marched on towards Preston all the while encountering hostile
bands of militia, some armed with nothing more than a pitchfork. By
the 10th of November they had reached Preston but were disappointed
by the lack of English support. But there was an even bigger problem
General Willis had a Hanoverian force ready comprising of one
regiment of infantry and five new regiments of dragoons. Forster was a
weak nervous man, who left everything to Borlum's supervision.
Stevenson has him tagged as a "non-entity, lacking any military skill,
self seeking and a coward"[383] Derwentwater on the other hand was the
exact opposite". The Jacobites managed to hold Preston for a short
time erecting barricades at the four main roads and turning houses into
strongholds. Forester was left to man the bridge over the Ribble but he
failed obviously not realizing the importance of this. This provided the
enemy with a clear road and Willis's men attacked on the 12th
November but Borlum had fortified Preston well enough to hold them
back. The following day a second force arrived under General
Carpenter. Preston was surrounded. The Jacobites could not hold out
for ever and there was no way out, the only alternative was to
surrender. Approximately 75 English and 145 Scottish noblemen and
gentlemen surrendered with around 1,300 ordinary soldiers. 200
English were killed with only 17 on the Jacobite side. Borlum
surrendered and was held in London for six months or thereabouts. He
made good his escape with six others and a price tag of £1,000 on his
head. Borlum ended up in France where he still fought with tenacity
for the Jacobite cause. He later fought in the 1719 rising but was later
caught, imprisoned at Edinburgh where he died a few years later.
Borlum was a true and faithful Jacobite who has been neglected by
some historians in the past. The Jacobites overall suffered only forty
casualties compared to the Hanoverians who had two hundred. Unlike
Dunkeld the attacking force where not going to disintegrate and leave.
This was the end of the Jacobite rising in England.

---

[382] R E Hutchison *The Jacobite Rising of 1715* (1965, p 24)
[383] C S Stevenson *Inglorious Rebellion The Jacobite Risings of 1708, 1717 and 1719*
(1973, p 139)

As a matter of interest, around 1771 a Jacobite club was founded at Preston called The Oyster and Parched Pea Club however, the meetings were more convivial than political[384]. The members, twelve in number, would meet at their houses with a barrel of oysters, brandy and claret. The club continued their meetings till 1841. A similar club was founded in Edinburgh in 1772 called The Royal Oak Club. This is probably how the acorn became known as a secret Jacobite symbol which was engraved on wine glasses and other artifacts.

Sheriffmuir (13th November 1715)

Borlum had surrendered at Preston while Mar still had a vastly superior force of between seven thousand and twelve thousand men, compared to Argyle's three thousand five hundred in Scotland. Argyles army consisted of five regiments of dragoons and eight foot battalions. What is not commonly known is the fact that many of Mars men were from the Lowlands, dressed in their plain grey doublets and breeches with blue bonnets[385]. Argyle had so little an army because the majority of the British forces were fighting in Flanders. Weeks had passed by, and the Earl of Mar had done virtually nothing. It could be argued that he was waiting for more clans to gather to the Standard[386]. However, this would be a weak argument for his indecisiveness. Eventually Mar moved his men from Perth to Sheriffmuir, Argyle was waiting in Dunblain. On the 13th November the two opposing armies lined up on the undulating Sheriffmuir[387]. However, the two forces were misaligned. Both armies outflanked each other on their right side. Argyle, however, was a man of tactics choosing ground far better suited to his infantry and dragoons than the Highlanders. He knew that the ground to the right was marshland but he did not know it had frozen over with the cold weather[388]. Mar had chosen the Highlanders as the first line to charge Argyle. They were in a two or three line

[384] Sir Charles Petrie *The Jacobite Movement The last phase 1716-1807* (1950, p 168-169)
[385] C S Stevenson *Inglorious Rebellion The Jacobite Risings of 1708, 1717 and 1719* (1973, p 148)
[386] J MacLehose *Scottish History & Life* (Graham, 1902, p 151)
[387] D Smurthwaite *The Complete Guide to the Battlefield of Britain* (1984, p 197)
[388] H Kemp *The Jacobite Rebellion* (1975, p 46)

formation and when they charged at Argyle's soldiers they drove back their left wing, which then panicked and ran. Mar and the Highlanders were then in hot pursuit. Highland tactics were always the same, charge at the enemy, fire their muskets and pistols then continue the charge through the smoke into the enemy lines. Muskets fired and swords slashed and stabbed in a flurry of cold steel. At the same time Argyle's army had held Mars left wing. Argyle's cavalry then charged and helped Argyle's right wing. The Highlanders began to retreat back to the Allan Water, still trying to rally together. After three hours or so Mars left wing was scattered. Both armies had lost their left wing to the opposing army's right wing. At this point of the battle neither army could see what had happened to their lost left wing because of the spread of men and the terrain.

Both armies' returned to the field of battle and for a few hours there was little activity between them. Mar still vastly outnumbered Argyle having approximately four thousand men to Argyles one thousand. If Mar had charged again, Argyle arguably would have been finished. Gordon of Glenbucket was apparently heard to groan "Oh for an hour of Dundee" The great Claverhouse would not have hesitated- and lost"[389]. Argyle seeing he was vastly outnumbered still managed to obtain a strong strategic position behind some turf walls[390]. With darkness looming ahead Mar went off to Ardoch, while Argyle went to Dunblain picking up his lost stragglers from the battle. In the morning Argyle marched back to Sheriffmuir, but the Highlanders were gone. Mar's booty consisted of "a quantity of military booty including four colours and 1,400 or 1,500 stand of arms[391]", Mar claimed the victory. Argyll "captured fourteen colours, five cannon and, most important, the Jacobite supply wagons"[392], Argyll claimed the victory as well. In early December approximately six thousand troops were sent over from the Dutch to help the Hanoverian succession. James came over to Scotland in early January, staying only a few weeks. Like the Earl of

---

[389] C S Stevenson *Inglorious Rebellion The Jacobite Risings of 1708, 1717 and 1719* (1973, p 156)
[390] R E Hutchison National Galleries of Scotland *The Jacobite Rising of 1715* (1965, p 27)
[391] R E Hutchison *ibid* (1965, p 27)
[392] R E Hutchison *ibid* (1965, p 27)

Mar he was no great leader[393], in fact he became known as Old melancholy. Nor did James have the personality traits that his son forth coming Prince Charles displayed later on in Scotland[394]. The Jacobite army remained at Perth till the 30th January 1716. It was then decided to march to Montrose stopping at Dundee. Argyles army had grown in strength and it was agreed it was not safe for James to stay in Scotland. Approximately £15,000 of Spanish gold was sent to Scotland by ship from Calais. Unfortunately the ship was wrecked of the coast of St Andrews with all the gold salvaged by the Hanoverians, the crew escaped. Not long after this and without informing their army James with the Earls of Mar, Melfort and Lord Drummond[395] amongst others sailed off to France on board the *Marie Thérèse* of St Malo[396] leaving their army to their own fate. This only added to the resentment that James had acquired from the Jacobite soldiers with his stay in Perth.

An anonymous writer of the time wrote "When we saw the man whom they called our King, we found ourselves not at all animated by his presence; if he was disappointed in us, we were tenfold more so in him. We saw nothing in him that looked the spirit. He never appeared with cheerfulness or vigour to animate us. Our men began to despise him; some asked if he could speak"[397]. James spent the rest of his life in exile. The Jacobites deserted by their leaders made their way to the hills once more.

---

[393] W M Mackenzie *Outline of Scottish History* (1916, p 399)
[394] R E Hutchison National Galleries of Scotland *The Jacobite Rising of 1715* (1965, p 11)
[395] H Brown *A Short History of Scotland* (1951, p 29)
[396] B Lenman *The Jacobite Cause* (1986, p 58)
[397] C S Stevenson *Inglorious Rebellion The Jacobite Risings of 1708, 1717 and 1719* (1973, p 165) Stevenson's footnote reads "The author of this tract never revealed his real name, but preferred to masquerade under the hardly debatable nom de plume or de guerre of "A Rebel". Some authorities have credited the writing to the Master of Stair, others to Daniel Defoe".
In my opinion it was more than likely Defoe since he was full of political schemes and an agent of the Hanoverian Government. There were spies all over Britain Jacobite and Hanoverian, male and female, one woman called A Lewis was particularly disreputable and of low moral fibre. Monod *Jacobitism and the English people, 1688-1788* (1993, p213)

Both sides claimed a victory but, in truth if anyone was victorious it was Argyle. He was vastly outnumbered yet he still prevented Mar from taking the Lowlands. Some six hundred of Argyles men were killed with Mar loosing around the same amount of men. The two most prominent noblemen who were caught and then executed in London were the Earl of Derwentwater[398] who was a cousin of James Francis Edward Stuart and Lord Kenmure[399]. Other prisoners were put on trial by an English jury and many thought it would be unfair but, with no executions handed out it was believed to be a fair trial. One of the reasons for the unbiased trial may be the fact that Duncan Forbes would not go to Carlisle to prosecute his countrymen because it was under an English jury and illegal[400]. In the meantime wealthy sympathizers gave the prisoners money, food and drink. Forester escaped prison by bribing the turnkeys and managing to get Governor Pitt inebriated. He managed to obtain duplicate keys and walked out the prison onto the streets of London, later to make his way to Paris. In 1717 an Act of Grace was given with a pardon to many Scots still in prison, they were subsequently released[401]. Unfortunately for the English Jacobites many were transported to plantations with twenty two being hanged in Lancashire. It is more than likely that if Mar retained his position as Secretary of State for Scotland someone else would have started the rising. Mar like Dundee, had previously been a supporter to William and he had also helped secure George I onto the throne.

The battle of Glenshiel (10th June 1719)

Hostilities between England and Spain were strained to breaking point. The English were "bound by the Treaty of Utrecht, signed in 1713 to guarantee Imperial territory in Italy[402]". George Bing was commissioned with twenty ships to restore peace in the Mediterranean.

[398] H Kemp *The Jacobite Rebellion* (1975, p 46)

[399] H Brown *A Short History of Scotland* (1951, p 296)

[400] C D Murray *Duncan Forbes of Culloden* (1936, p 6)

[401] R E Hutchison National Galleries of Scotland *The Jacobite Rising of 1715* (1965, p 31)

[402] C S Stevenson *Inglorious Rebellion The Jacobite Risings of 1708, 1717 and 1719* (1973, p 213)

If that failed then his mission was to try and obstruct any Spanish hostility. Spain retaliated by seizing any English ships that were in their ports. A new dual strategy was arranged between Philip V of Spain and the Jacobite James Butler, Duke of Ormonde who would take command[403]. Spain would supply five warships and twenty two frigates with five thousand men and a huge quantity of arms. A smaller force of two frigates holding mainly exiled Jacobites and three hundred Spanish infantry left heading for Scotland under the command of George Keith, arriving on 13th April on the West coast. There duty was to incite and fuel another rising in Scotland. The larger force sailing for England encountered a severe storm on the 8th March[404] near Cape Finisterre and thus abandoned the venture. Keith met up with a few Scottish noblemen, the Earl of Seaforth and the Marquis of Tullibardine. News of the abandoned fleet reached the Highlanders, and, therefore only a thousand or so men rallied to the call. Meanwhile General Wightman had eleven hundred troops marching to meet them. The troops were mainly from the Inverness area with support from Whig clans Munro, Ross and MacKay. Sir Robert Munroe was out of the country but his younger brother who was a captain assembled some of the Munro clan[405]. They marched with the regular troops to Glenshiel where the battle lasted for nearly three hours. At last the Jacobites left wing was broken, and then Wightman concentrated his assault on the Spanish troops who were in the centre. The Spaniards were resolutely brave but to retreat and make haste with the Highlanders was impractical for them. At the advice of the Jacobite leaders the Spanish infantry who had stood fast surrendered. The Highlanders disappeared to the hills again and the Earl of Seaforth and others made peace with the Government. There were little losses on both sides which is surprising. The Hanoverians sustaining around twenty men killed with one hundred and twenty wounded. The Jacobites had somewhere in the region of eighty men killed these

---

[403] D Smurthwaite *The Complete Guide to the Battlefield of Britain* (1984, p 200)
[404] Sir Charles Petrie *The Jacobite Movement The last phase 1716-1807* (1950, p 23)
[405] P Doddridge *Some Remarkable Passages in the Life of the Honourable Col. James Gardiner who was slain at the Battle of Preston-pans. September 21st 1745 With an appendix relating to the Ancient Family of the Munro's of Fowlis.* (1764, p 206)

figures were confirmed by Keith later on[406]. The Hanoverians then plundered and burned Seaforth's territory before returning to Inverness. The Spanish prisoners (two hundred and seventy four of them) were taken to Inverness then Edinburgh but were later released through negotiations in October to return to Spain.

It was not until 1745 that any real attempt was made to regain the crown for the Stewarts by Bonnie Prince Charlie and a great deal has been said regarding brutality on the field of battle. However, one story again not in the scope of this book is mentioned by Johnson regarding honour during a battle[407]. "At [the battle of] Falkirk a gentleman now living was, I suppose after the retreat of the King's troops, engaged at a distance from the rest with an Irish dragoon. They were both skilled swordsmen, and the contest was not easily decided. The dragoon at last had the advantage, and the Highlander called for quarter; but quarter was refused him, and the fight continued till he was reduced to defend himself upon his knee. At that instant one of the Macleods came to his rescue who , as it is said, offered quarter to the dragoon, but he thought himself obliged to reject what he had before refused, and as battle gives little time to deliberate, was immediately killed".

Highlanders would customarily carry their firearms, sword and target on any travels whether it was the local market or church, their dirk of course would always be at hands reach. Even in the Lowlands a Gentleman would carry a sword to indicate his social status. All this changed after 1746, true there had been various attempts in the past with Disarming Acts but these were in one way or another avoided by the Highlanders. The subjugation after Culloden in 1746 ensured the old Highland warrior way of life was finished.

---

[406] C S Stevenson *Inglorious Rebellion The Jacobite Risings of 1708, 1717 and 1719* (1973, p 231)
[407] Samuel Johnson *A journey to the Western Islands of Scotland* (1773, p 171-172)

Appendix 1

Tartan

By Gordon Nicolson

Tartan originates from the French word 'Tiretaine' which translated into Gaelic simply means 'Breacan' (striped cloth).Tartan is a woollen cloth which is woven with a shuttle on a loom. The origin of tartan is not exactly known, however. In my opinion tartan can be traced back to Roman times where evidence of a basic simple check has been found. It is important to set the scene for tartan. In my view, the development of tartan can be broken into two eras, namely, pre 1746 (after the battle of Culloden) and the early 1800S.

The Pre 1746 period

In order to make tartan the process was as follows. The long fleecy wool from a sheep would be cut and collected before moulting. The fleece was bagged and then stored until there was enough for the purpose intended. The dirty wool was cleaned in urine to remove grease and other impurities. It was spun, and then dyed by using local plants, vegetables and minerals that make the unique colours to weave the cloth. The Scots did not have access to large dying vats hence why there were more colours and less quantity.

Weaving was an art form and great pride was taken in the closeness of the weave and designs that were produced. Tartan was woven more by the women than men. Weaving tartan was a painstaking task which was diligently accomplished by using the thread counts marked on a stick. Hence the first district tartans (as one knows them now) were woven and worn by a similar, named group of people.

In reality, the stick would have been probably used as a guide for the set. The richer people would be able to afford the rich and colourful tartans. The poorer folk would have to make do with what they had.

The colours at this time could not be easily replicated as the dying process was subject to many variants.

After the Battle of Culloden in 1746 the Disarming Act was passed in 1747. Within the Act there was a prohibition to the effect that: "Any persons within Scotland, whether man or boy (excepting officers and soldiers in his majesty's service), who should wear the plaid, philibeg, trews, shoulder belts, or any part of the Highland garb, or should use for great coats, tartans, or parti-coloured plaid, or stuffs, should, without the alternative of a fine, be imprisoned for the first conviction for six months, without bail, and on the second conviction be transported for seven years"[408]. Therefore, from 1746 until the early 1800s, much culture and traditions were lost.

The Disarming Act was repealed in 1782. The Lowlanders, in particular women, took to wearing the tartan which was still seen as a sign of rebellion. Obviously, there was a large industry simply bubbling away just waiting to be unleashed. Whilst the Act was intended to suppress rebellion, the Act did give us the tartan which we are familiar with today. More importantly, the Act, in a strange kind of way, gave us our national identity. Without the Act the wearing of tartan would simply have been confined to those living in the Highlands. The importance of the Act was that it had the effect of making the wearing of tartan both generally desirable and also a symbol of 'Scottishness'.

Early 1800s to the present

Sir Walter Scott is responsible for the visit of King George IV in 1822 to Scotland. He was the first king to visit Scotland since Culloden. Scott, through his writing and storytelling, had glamorised tartan and the highlands. The King also wore tartan for the visit and this left clan chiefs clambering to get their clan tartans for the royal visit. This caused the biggest surge of tartan weaving ever seen and mills were struggling to cope with the demand. The clan chiefs scrambled to Wilsons of Bannockburn and other mills to choose their clan tartan from the vast array of sample books which they kept. This is why there are so many tartans that are similar in colour and sett. The

---

[408] http://www.electricscotland.com/history/highland_dress.htm

mills were so busy that they sold every piece of tartan that was made Originally, Wilsons used the 'stick' method for producing recorded tartan septs and then they introduced the 'SINDEX' method which is still used today for the recording of tartan. This method numbers and identifies each tartan so that it could be reproduced almost exactly on a commercial basis.

Hence, clan tartans had arrived. Tartan has now developed over the years. With the advent of chemical dyes there are many more colours which the tartan weaver has at his disposal. Modern tartans, and dress tartans which followed, were aimed predominantly at women. Tartan nowadays has four colour options, that is to say, weathered, muted, ancient, and modern. In some cases two tartans are merged to produce one tartan. The correct way to describe this type of tartan is to name the tartan first and then name the colour way which distinguishes the colours. One such example is the Nicolson Hunting Muted tartan.

In conclusion, tartan has evolved over the years and is indeed, continually changing. The introduction of the World Tartan Register has enabled a single body to oversee and develop the standards of the vast introduction of new tartans.

Appendix 2

The following tartans have Jacobite connections mostly through written accounts. These tartans are related to as district tartans more than anything else. As mentioned earlier in (chapter 3) with conviction there was no clan connection relating to tartan in the 17th and 18th century. Further proof is given by Alexander MacDonald, the Gaelic poet, who related "how it was impossible to distinguish his own clan Ranald MacDonalds from other MacDonalds"[409]. However, bodies of men did adopt and wear tartan to probably distinguish themselves from others. "In 1713 the Royal Company of Archers, the Queens bodyguard in Scotland adopted tartan as their uniform"[410], so did the Black watch. The Queens bodyguard may have adopted the tartan as a symbol of their anti Union feelings or Jacobite sympathies. Paradoxically not all Highland gentlemen wore tartan with regularity and some Lowland gentlemen did wear tartan[411].

The colours in these tartans are perhaps similar to the muted colours that we have nowadays. Although it must be said that the Highlanders did have a love for exuberant colour and this is evident in surviving tartans from the period which will have faded over the years. Modern tartan is subject to a chemical dying process that simply did not exist back in the old days.

Caledonia tartan was popular in the 18th century; it is linked with the Jacobites although it must be said romantically.

Culloden tartan, this tartan obviously bears its name from the battle fought on Drummossie Moor 16th April 1746. One of the Princes officers is reportedly to have worn a coat made from this tartan, found on the Moor after the battle.

---

[409] H Cheape *Tartan* 2nd edition National Museums of Scotland (1992, p 72)
[410] C Hesketh *Tartans* (1972, p 22)
[411] C Hesketh *ibid* (1972, p 12)

Dunblain tartan, this tartan is said to be taken from a portrait painted in the first quarter of the 18th century. The portrait was of the 2nd Viscount of Dunblain who died in 1729.

Huntley tartan, this tartan is probably one of the most authentic tartans known and associated with the Jacobite cause. Many clansmen are reputed to have worn it during the 1745-46 Rising from Gordon, Ross, Brodie, Forbes and Munro. An individual from the MacRae clan is said to have worn the tartan during the 1715 rising. Prince Charles is said to have worn the tartan in a slight variation during the 45.

Lennox tartan, this is probably the oldest tartan on record and is said to have connections with Mary Queen of Scots. This would connect it with the second half of the 16th century.

Sutherland tartan, this tartan is very similar to the tartan associated with the Campbells during the 18th century. Before 1745-46 various portraits have certain Campbells in reddish tartan. What was known as Black Watch tartan is now known as Campbell tartan, the connection was probably through Campbell Militia during the 45[412].

I would like to mention that the book *District Tartans* by Teall of Teallach and Smith (1992) has been heavily sourced for information in this appendix. For a more in-depth study of District tartans I would recommend their work.

---

[412]H F McClintock & J T Dunbar *Old Highland Dress and Tartans* (1949, P 76)

142

Appendix 3

The materials and dying process's in the 17th and 18th century from MacKay's *Highland Garb & the Tartan* (1924).

Black No 1, Alder tree bark.

Process: Boil the bark for a few hours then remove the exhausted dye material, add a little chrome with the wool and boil for a half hour or until the wool reaches the required depth of colour. If the process is done without the chrome a brown colour will be the result.

Black No 2, Dock root with the same process.

Black No 3, Water flag root without the chrome and only boiled for half an hour.

Brown No 1, Tops of current bushes and alum.

Process: Boil the current branches for two hours then add the alum and wool boil for a further half hour.

Brown No 2, Blaeberry with gall nuts boil till the colour develops.

Blue No 1, Elder with alum

Process: Boil together with the wool for one or two hours according to the shade required.

Blue No 2, Blaeberry with alum, boil ingredients with the wool for one or two hours according to the shade required.

Purple No 1, Tops cut from heather.

Process: Boil the heather tops for two hours then remove when the colour is exhausted. Add one ounce of alum for every pound of raw wool and boil for a further half hour.

Purple No 2, Sundew plants

Process: Boil for one or two hours with the wool depending on the depth of colour required.

Violet, Wild cress

Process: Boil for one to two hours with the wool.

Red No 1, White crotal.

Process: The crotal is first dried out under the sun then powdered down. The powder is then steeped in urine in an air tight vessel for three weeks. It is then boiled with the wool for one to two hours according to the shade required.

Red No 2, Rue root.

Process: Boil the roots for two hours then add the wool and boil till the colour develops.

Green dark Ash tree root.

Boil the root for two hours then remove the roots. Add a little chrome with the wool and boil for a further half an hour. If the chrome is not added a yellow colour will be given.

Green light, Knapweed.

Process: Boil the plant tops with the roots, wool and a little alum till the required shade is developed.

Green No 3, Broom.

Process: Boil the broom for two to three hours then extract the dye. Add the wool and boil till colour is required.

Whin bark or Fuller thistle can be used with the same process above.

Dark grey, Root of yellow flag.

Process: Boil the roots for half an hour then remove the roots. Add a little chrome with the wool and boil for a further half hour.

Yellow No 1, Bog myrtle.

Process: Boil the plant for two hours then remove, add the wool and boil till colour is developed.

Yellow No 2, St John's wort.

Process: Same as above.

Orange dark, Bramble bush.

Process: Boil with the wool till colour develops.

Flesh colour, Willow bark.

Process: Boil the bark for two hours then extract the bark. Add the wool and boil till the required shade is developed.

Magenta, Dandelion,

Process Boil the plant for two hours, remove the plants and add the wool, boil for a half hour.

Appendix 4

The following mottos and inscriptions are to be found on door lintels, (whether they are still present would require further research) daggers, dirks, swords and powder horns of Scottish manufacture. The inscriptions that are dated seem to be from the middle of the 16th to the late 17th century.

The following is on a two handed sword

I Will Venter Selfe In Batel Strong

ToVindicate My Masters Wroing:

The following inscription is on a brass sporran clasp

Open my mouth, cut not my skin.

And then you'll see what is Therin:

The following is etched on a dirk blade and dated to around the late 17th century

Thy King and Countries Cause Defend Though On The Spot Your Life Should End and *A Soft Ansuer Tourneth Away Wrath:*

The following inscriptions are on powder horns and daggers.

My Treist is in Ye Lord:

God Gyde The Hand That I Instand:

My Hop and Trest is In Ye Lord:

Al Mi Hope Is In Ye Lord:

O Lord God Be My Defender:

Ask Me Not for Shame Drink Lis And By Ane:

In God Is My Trust:

O Lord In Ye Is All My Trust:

O Lord In The Is Al My Traist:

On a door lintel in the High Street of Edinburgh is the following

In The Lord Is My Hope 1564:

On a door lintel in Blackfriars Wynd in Edinburgh is

In Domine Speravi . O Lord I Put My Trust In Thee. 1619:

Be My Defens God Defend Forever More:

The timber fronted gables of Huntly House in the Canongate have the following inscriptions translated from Latin:

Another hope of life.

To a constant spirit the things of mortals

Are as a shadow.

As you are master of your tongue, so

Am I master of my ears.

To-day for me, to-morrow for you, why worry? 1570

Captain Burt also noticed the custom of some gentlemanly folk inscribing their initials presumably on stone work outside their house. Others had their initials with a piece of their poetry on stonework near the chimney, here are his two examples:

16 WMB As with the Fire, EMP 94

So with thy God do stand;

Keep not far off, Nor come too near Hand

The other is:

16 Christ is my life and rent, 78

His promise is evident

LS   HF

When Burt was quartered in the Lowlands he pointed out that few Public houses have signs above the door indicating it to be a tavern held by a person of distinction. In Burt's narrative "I have seen written upon several--------Mr. *Alexander* or Mr. *James* such a one; this is a token that the Man of the House is a Gentleman either by birth, or that he has taken his Master of Arts Degree at the University"[413].

Inscribed on a dirk of the late 17th century is the motto

Fear God and Do Not Kill 1680:

On flat powder horns the following inscriptions have been found.

Seck Me Not I Pray The My Master Vil Deney Me Fatles Apryl 4 Year Of God 1694 And. Booy. Fear God In Heat:

On a powder horn written in Latin are the words

Memorandvm Nvlli Dandvm Ob Cavsam QdDam Non Sciendam Nec Rogandam Jvne 2nd and on the same horn Gift Livetenand William Grant Of Advie To Iohn Donaldsone Of Bogsyde 169:

William Turners powder horn reads

William Tvrner 1677 and *Sike Me Vithin Pouder*:

On another powder horn

I Love Thee As My Wyffe

I'll Keep Thee As My Lyffe

---

[413] Edward Burt *Letters from a Gentleman in the North of Scotland to His Friend in London* Volume 1 (1754, p 81)

On the same horn with the date *1689* are the words

A Man His Mynd Should Never Set

Upon A Thing He Can Not Get:

On a powerhorn is the date with the owners' name

1723 IAMES INOS and on the reverse side

A whiter horn ye do not ken

Appendix 5

The majority of maker's marks or marks of origin are generally stamped in the fuller or fullers of the blade, very few examples are dated.

ANDREA FERRARA

Often spelt with variations;

AN DR EA on either side of the blade *FA RA RA*

· SS· ANDRIA · SS·

· SS· FARARA · SS·

X ANDRIA X FARARA X

X) I (X XIIX X) I (X: ANDRIA X FARARA: X) I (X XIIX X) I (X

ANDRIA on one side and on the other *FARARA*

[A]NDR[EA]   [F]ARA[A]

FERARA SAHAHVN ON THE OTHER SIDE FERARA ELVIEHO

[AND]RIA XX

The list is quite exhaustive but it does help give an idea of how many different Ferrara blades were being made. Other maker's marks from the Solingen region are signed in Latin form;

JACOB/BRACH and on the other side *MEFECIT/SOLINGEN*

ME FECIT/HERMMEN KEISER/SOLINGEN

WILHELM WIRSBERGH NE FECIT SOLINGEN

CORNELIVS WVNDES SOLINGEN FECIT

Other swordsmith's who signed their blades from the Solingen region are;

Jacob Brach, 1650

Caspar Carn Solingen 1610-1630 and London from *1630-?*

From the Wundes family there is;

Johann Wundes 1590-1625

Cornelis Wundes 1650

Matthias Wundes 1580

Again this list is exhaustive and only a few have been added to this appendix.

It is obvious in (Appendix 3 & 4) that various sources of old contemporary writings used different spellings to describe mottos, inscriptions or the occurrence of events. This was probably due to certain factors "wide spread illiteracy and the general lack of rationalized written language"[414], this is evident in Scotland, England and probably all over Europe.

Norman C Milne Copyright © 2010

---

[414] J Walter *The sword and bayonet makers of Imperial Germany 1871-1918* (1973, p 8)

Bibliography

J Anderson & J Drummond (1881) *Ancient Scottish Weapons* George Waterston & Sons Edinburgh and London

T R Barnett (1942) *Scottish Pilgrimage in the Land of Lost Content* John Grant booksellers Limited Edinburgh

M Barrington (1911) *Grahame of Claverhouse Viscount Dundee* Martin Secker, London

D Baxandall National Galleries of Scotland *The Jacobite Rising of 1715* (1965)

H Brown (1951) *A Short History of Scotland* Oliver & Boyd Ltd Edinburgh

R Burns (1990) *The Complete Illustrated Poems' Songs & Ballads of Robert Burns* 3rd edition Lomond books

E Burt (1754) *Letters from a Gentleman in the North of Scotland to His Friend in London*

D Butler (1906) *The Tron Kirk of Edinburgh* or *Christ's Kirk at the Tron*. Oliphant, Anderson & Ferrier Edinburgh & London

D H Caldwell (1979) *The Scottish Armoury.* William Blackwood

Caldwell D H (1981) *Scottish Weapons & Fortifications 1100-1800.* John Donald Publishers Ltd

Lord Archibald Campbell (1899) *Highland Dress, Arms and Ornament.* London

Campsie A K (1980) *The MacCrimmon Legend.* Edinburgh Canongate

R W Chapman *Johnson & Boswell A journey to the Western Islands of Scotland* and *The journal of a tour to the Hebrides* (1974) Oxford University Press

H Cheape (1995) *Tartan* 2nd edition National Museums of Scotland

P Cochrane (1987) *Scottish Military Dress*. Blandford Press London, New York, Sydney

M Craig (1977) *Damn' Rebel Bitches The Women of the '45*. Mainstream publishing Edinburgh and London.

Culloden the Swords and the Sorrows (1996) An exhibition to commemorate the Jacobite Rising of 1745 and the Battle of Culloden 1746. Published by The National; Trust for Scotland Company Ltd

V Dolinek J Durdik (1993) The *encyclopedia of European Historical Weapons*. Hamlyn publications

P Doddridge (1764) *Some Remarkable Passages in the Life of the Honourable Col. James Gardiner who was slain at the Battle of Preston-pans. September 21st 1745 With an appendix relating to the Ancient Family of the Munro's of Fowlis*. Printed for John Orr and sold first shop above Gibson's Wynd Glasgow.

David Johnson *Music and Society in Lowland Scotland in the Eighteenth Century* (1972) Oxford University Press

J T Dunbar   (1979) *History of Highland Dress* B.T Batsford Ltd London

J T Dunbar (1984) *The Costume of Scotland*. B T Batsford Ltd London

J T Dunbar *Orkney Miscellany Orkney Record and Antiquary Society*, Volume 1 p 201 (1953)

L A Dunkling *Scottish Christian Names* 2nd edition (1988) Published by Johnston & Bacon Books Ltd Stirling

J D Foreman (1993) *The Scottish Dirk* Historical Arms Series No 26. Printed in Canada for Museum Restoration Service

M Francisque *The Scottish Language as illustrated Civilisation in Scotland* (1882) William Blackwood and Sons Edinburgh & London

A Fulton (1991) *Scotland and her Tartans* Hodder Stoughton, London Sydney Auckland

A D Gibb (1950) *Law from over the Border* Edinburgh

E Goldsmid (1885) *The Massacre of Glencoe 13th of February 1692 Being A Reprint of that a Contemporary Account of that Ruthless Butchery.* E. & G. Goldsmid, Edinburgh

H G Graham (1928) *The Social Life of Scotland in the Eighteenth Century.* A & C Black Ltd. London

Francis Grose (1801) *Military Antiquities* Respecting A History of the English Army, Volume 1, London

K & D Guest (1996) *British Battles* English Heritage Harper Collins Publishers

I Hamilton QC (1994) *A Touch More Treason* Neil Wilson publishing Glasgow Scotland

C Hesketh (1972) *Tartans*, 2nd edition Octopus books Ltd London

R E Hutchison (1965) *The Jacobite Rising of 1715* Scottish National Portrait Gallery Edinburgh

Sir Thomas Innes of Learney Lord Lyon King of Arms (1956) *Scots Heraldry* Printed by R. & R. Clark, Ltd Edinburgh

Sir Thomas Innes of Learney Lord Lyon King of Arms (1964) *The Tartans of the Clans and Families of Scotland* W. & A. K. Johnston & G. W. Bacon Ltd, Edinburgh and London

Samuel Johnson *A Journey to the Western Islands of Scotland in 1773* Reprinted in 1908 Preface by D.T. Holmes B.A. Paisley Alexander Gardner

H Kemp (1975) *The Jacobite Rebellion* Almark publishing Co Ltd London

Sir G Laking (1904) *The Armoury of Windsor Castle* London

Lang Syne Publishers (1992) *Scottish Battles* Printed by David Barr Printers

R W Latham (1977) *Antique Guns in colour 1250-186* Blandford Press Ltd

B Lenman (1980) *The Jacobite Risings in Britain 1689-1756* Printed by Willmer Brothers Ltd Rockferry Merseyside

B Lenman (1986) *The Jacobite Cause*. Richard Drew Publishing in association with National Trust for Scotland

R D Lobban *The Clansmen* (1969) University of London Press Ltd

D M Macdonald (1964) *Scotland's magazine and Scottish Country Life*
The Armourers of Glen Lyon Volume 60 No 6 June 1964

Neil MacGregor (1998) *John Roy Stuart: Jacobite Bard of Strathspey* An extract from Volume LXIII of the Gaelic Society of Inverness

J G MacKay (1924) *The Romantic Story of the Highland Garb and the Tartan*. With an Appendix by Lieut.-Colonel Norman MacLeod G.M.G., D.S.O., publisher Eneas Mackay Stirling

W MacKay Junior (1930) *Some notes on Highland weapons*. Netherwood Inverness

W C Mackenzie (1934) *Lovat of the Forty-five* The Moray Press
Edinburgh & London

W M Mackenzie (1916) *Outline of Scottish History* A. & C. Black, Ltd
London

A Mackie (1967) *Scottish Pageantry* Hutchison & Co publishers Ltd

R Mackie (1947) *A Short History of Scotland* Oxford University Press

John Macky (1729) *A Journey Through Scotland* Publisher J
Pemberton and J Hooke

Maclean F., (1995) *Highlanders A History of the Highland Clans*
David
Campbell Publishers Limited.

J MacLehose (1902) *Scottish History & Life* James MacLehose &
Sons, publishers to the University Glasgow

Martin Martin (1703) *A Description of the Western Islands of Scotland
Circa 1695/ A Voyage to St Kilda* with *A Description of the Occidental
i.e. Western Islands of Scotland* by Donald Monro Introduction by E J
Withers & R W Munro (1999) published by Birlinn Limited
Edinburgh

S Maxwell & R Hutchison (1958) *Scottish Costume 1550-1850.*
London Adam & Charles Black

S Maxwell T B Lindsay C Blair J Wallace W Reid J G Scott A V B
Norman (1963) *Scottish Weapons The Scottish Art Review Magazine*
published by the Glasgow Art Gallery and Museums Association.
Volume 9 No 1, 1963

P K Monod *Jacobitism and the English people, 1688-1788* (1993)
Cambridge University Press

H F McClintock J T Dunbar (1949) *Old Highland Dress and Tartans* W Tempest Dundalgan Press, Dundalk

R R McIan (1845) *Costumes of the Clans of Scotland* with descriptive letterpress by James Logan London Ackerman and Co, Strand

W Moffat (1985) *A History of Scotland*, book 4. Oxford University Press

Rev. Thomas Morer (1702) *A Short Account of Scotland. Being a description of the Nature of that Kingdom, and what the Constitution of it is in Church and State, wherin also some notice is taken of their Chief Cities of Royal Boroughs, with an Appendix about their Kings Supremacy, the difference of the Scotch and English Liturgy. The Revenue and Expence on the Civil and Military List, according to a late Establishment* London Reprinted London (1715) as *A Short Account of Scotland, etc* Written by the late Rev. Mr Thomas Morer, Minister of St Ann's Within Aldersgate When he was Chaplan to a Scots Regiment"

A E Mowbray (1971) Lord Archibald Campbell *Scottish Swords from the Battlefield at Culloden*. Printed by Mowbray Company-Publishers, Providence Rhode Island

C D Murray (1936) *Duncan Forbes of Culloden* International Publishing Company London

J I W Murray (1934) *Scotland through the ages* Part 2 McDougall's Educational Co Ltd Edinburgh London

W H Murray (1982) *Rob Roy MacGregor His life and Times* Canongate Books Ltd Edinburgh

A V B Norman (1962) *The Journal of The Arms & Armour Society Early Military Dirks in the Scottish United Services Museum*, Edinburgh Volume IV No 1 March 1962

Oliver & Boyd (1929) *Edinburgh 1329-1929* Tweeddale Court Edinburgh

J Paton (1896) *Scottish National Memorials* Published by James MacLehose and Sons, publishers to the University

Sir Charles Petrie (1950) *The Jacobite Movement The last phase 1716-1807.* Eyre & Spottiswood publishers Ltd London

Sir Charles Petrie (1958) *The Stuarts* 2nd edition Eyre & Spottiswood publishers Ltd London

Dr. Tony Pollard & Neil Oliver (2003) *Two Men in a Trench II Uncovering the secrets of British Battlefields* Penguin books.

The Porcelli Barron (1949) *The White Cockade* Second Edition Printed by Anchor Press Ltd. Tiptree Essex

J Prebble (1973) *Glencoe* Penguin Books Ltd. made and printed in Great Britain by Hazel Watson & Viney Ltd, Aylesbury

J Prebble (1981) *The Lion in the North* Third edition Penguin books

Rev. T Thomson (1894) *A History of the Scottish People From the Earliest Times*, Volume V, Blackie & Son Ltd, London, Glasgow, Edinburgh and Dublin

Rae John (1895) *Life of Adam Smith* printed by Macmillan & Co London

T I Rae (1974) *The Union of 1707 It's impact on Scotland* Blackie and Son Ltd

B Robertson (1925) *Jacobite Activities in and around Inverness 1688-1746* printed by James Heap Ltd

M Rector *Highland Swordsmanship* (2001) from D McBane *The Expert Sword-man's Companion* (1728)

W Sacheverell (1702) *An account of the Isle of Man, with a Voyage to I-Columb-kill*

W Sandys & S A Forster (2006) *The History of the Violin (and other instruments played on with the bow from the remotest times to the present)* Dover Publications, INC. Mineola, New York Originally printed in London by William Reeves (1864)

Sir Walter Scot (1893) *Rob Roy The Waverly Novels* Dryburgh edition Volume IV. London and Edinburgh, Adam and Charles Black

R T Skinner (1947) The *Royal Mile* Oliver & Boyd Edinburgh

Sir Thomas Innes of Learney Lord Lyon King of Arms (1956) *Scots Heraldry* Printed by R. & R. Clark, Ltd Edinburgh

Sir Thomas Innes of Learney Lord Lyon King of Arms (1964) *The Tartans of the Clans and Families of Scotland* W. & A. K. Johnston & G. W. Bacon Ltd, Edinburgh and London

D Smurthwaite (1984) the complete Guide to the *Battlefields of Britain*. Published by the Penguin Group

M W Stuart (1952) *Old Edinburgh Taverns* Printed by J. and J. Grey, Edinburgh.

C S Stevenson (1973) *Inglorious Rebellion The Jacobite Risings of 1708, 1717 and 1719* Granada Publishing Limited Published by Panther books Ltd Park St, St Albans Herts

A Tayler & H Tayler (1930) *Jacobite Letters to Lord Pitsligo 1745-1746*. Aberdeen Milne & Hutchison

Teall & Smith (1992) *District Tartans* Shepheard-Walwyn (Publishers) Ltd

C W Thomson S (1909) *Scotland's Work and Worth*. Volume 1 Published by Oliphant, Anderson & Ferrier Edinburgh & London

John Wallace (1970) *Scottish Swords and Dirks* An illustrated reference guide to Scottish edged weapons. Arms and Armour Press

J Walter (1973) *The sword and bayonet makers of Imperial Germany 1871-1918* The Lyon Press Arms and Armour Press

P Warner (1976) *Famous Scottish Battles* Printed in Great Britain by William Collins & Co Ltd Glasgow

A Warrack (1988) *The Scots Dialect Dictionary* Lomond Books

L Weirter (1913) *The story of Edinburgh Castle* George G Harrap & Company Portsmouth Street Kingsway W.C. London

Charles E Whitelaw (1977) *Scottish Arms Makers* A biographical dictionary of makers of firearms, edged weapons and armour working in Scotland from the 15th Century to 1870. Arms and Armour Press

R M White & I D Willock (1999) *The Scottish Legal System* third edition Lexis Nexis Butterworths

F Wilkinson (1969) *Flintlock Pistols An illustrated Reference Guide to Flintlock Pistols from the 17th to the 19th Century* Arms & Armour Press

Websites

http://www.bayviewkentallen.co.uk/glencoemassacre.html

http://www.jedburgh-online.org.uk/history.asp

http://www.clan-cameron.org/battles/1690.html

http://www.donachiesociety.co.uk/history.html

http://www.scottish.parliament.uk/corporate/history/SPTradition/treaty
.htm

http://www.bbc.co.uk/history/historic_figures/anne_queen.shtml

http://www.royalinsight.org.uk/output/Page140.asp

http://en.wikipedia.org/wiki/Battle_of_Glen_Shiel

http://www.electricscotland.com/webclans/m/milne2.html

http://www.searchforancestors.com/surnames/origin/

http://www.1745association.org.uk/favourite_links_page.htm#Online
%20Links%20to%20useful%20Books

www.alba.org.uk/timeline/1707to1832.html

http://www.google.co.uk/Top/Regional/Europe/United_Kingdom/Scot
land/Aberdeen,_City_of/Arts_and_Entertainment/

http://www.contemplator.com/history/glencoe.html#top

http://www.electricscotland.com/History/nation/banff.htm

http://ourworld.compuserve.com/homepages/lenn
ich/history.htm

http://forejustice.org/wc/sp/scottish_pardons.html

http://www.geocities.com/scottishmoney/coins/postunion.html

http://www.geo.ed.ac.uk/home/scotland/saltire.html

http://www.fordham.edu/halsall/mod/lect/mod03.html

http://www.britannica.com/eb/topic-516741/University-of-Saint-Andrews

http://www.simmonsgallery.co.uk/2001site/tokens/MB38/Macmillan_Collection_Communion_Tokens-MB38.htm

http://www.chebucto.ns.ca/Heritage/FSCNS/Scots_NS/Clans/Henderson/Chief_Henderson/Chief_Henderson.html

http://www.electricscotland.com/history/glencoe/glen2.html

http://www.annongul.i12.com/page_11.htm

http://www.parliament.uk/actofunion/04_02_course.html

http://en.wikipedia.org/wiki/Daniel_Defoe.

http://www.standingstones.com/scot18th.html

http://www.clandavidsonusa.com/macphersonsrant.htm

http://www.pteratunes.org.uk/Music/Music/Lyrics/MacphersonsRant.html

http://scottishparodies.tripod.com/lyricsandfreesonglyrics/id6.html

http://news.scotsman.com/entertainment/Theatre-review-MacPherson39s-Rant-.5755365.jp

Author's biography

Norman Charles Milne was born in Edinburgh on the 21st July 1961. After leaving school at sixteen Norman went into the sheet-metal working industry. His father Charles bought him his first kilt at the age of nineteen and this helped inspire Norman on his trek through Scottish history. He soon started making sgian dubhs and sporrans as a hobby and registered with the Edinburgh Assay Office as a silversmith. His artistic accuracy for historic detail soon enabled him to open a shop in Edinburgh specializing in 17th and 18th century weapons and Highland dress of the period. Historical re-enactors and collectors were soon queuing to buy his dirks, targes, sporrans, swords and other accoutrements.

In 1999 Norman loaned the National Trust for Scotland three 18th century dirks for display at the Culloden Visitor Centre. Norman also takes part in re-enactment events throughout Scotland with the Circle of Gentlemen and Frasers Dragoons. He was recently in the new film about the Highland charge on Culloden Moor by the National Trust for Scotland and Neil Oliver's History of Scotland.

Normans academic achievements are LLB (Bachelor of Laws) and an MSc in (Business Management) from Edinburgh Napier University. Both degrees inspired Norman to write this book.

His other interests are the restoration of classic motorbikes, playing the violin and karate having taught adults and children for over twenty five years.

Index

Gypsies, 75

Halberds, 84
Hamilton of Bangour, 16
Hamilton, (Duke of), 57
Hamilton, I, 8
Hamilton, Lieutenant-Colonel, 120
Hamilton, Major General, 126
Hanoverians', 14,17,23,25,49,70,73,128,130,132,133,135136
Henchmen, 16, 35
Henderson, Clan, 120,121,123
Henderson, Francis, 108
Heraldry, 19, 20, 44
High Street, 32, 55, 58,103
Highland Line, 16, 23,27,28,50
Highlands (incl.Highlanders),
14,15,16,17,18,21,22,23,24,25,26,27,28,29,30,32,35,36,37,39,43,45,46,47,48,49,50,5
53,60,64,65,66,67,70,78,79,84,85,87,88,89,90,91,96,100,101,103,107,110,114,115,11
,122,123,124,125,127,129,131,132,135,136
Holland, 18, 24,44,52,67,111,113
Hope, William, 25
Hose or socks, 47, 55
Hospitality, 33, 36, 82,121
Huntly, Marques of, 127
Huts, 24, 28,121

Indians, 55,
Innkeepers, 23
Inverness, 21,35,67,68,69,90,97,101,111,116,127,128,135,136
Ireland, 37, 81,116,117,128
Italy, 26,126,134

Jacobites, 35,116,117,118,124,125,126,127,129,130,133,134,135
James, Richard, 97
Jedburgh Staff, 85, 86
Jenny Ha's, 32
Johnston, Samuel, 7, 25, 26,27,30,66

Keith, 75
Keith, George, 135,136
Kenmure, Viscount, 127,129
Kerchiefs, 51,
Killicrankie, 19, 25,115
Killicrankie, Battle of, 19, 72, 89,106,112

9 781899 820795